The Larger Faith

*Erected in 1792, the First Universalist Church in Oxford, MA, was the
likely site of the first Universalist general convention.*

The Larger Faith

A Short History of American Universalism

Charles A. Howe

Boston: Skinner House Books

Note: Every attempt has been made to avoid sexist and racist language in this book. In the interest of historical authenticity, the documents quoted are printed in their original form.

Throughout this book, references are made to the "merger" of the American Unitarian Association and the Universalist Church of America. Though the word merger is occasionally used, informally, in fact the two predecessor organizations were legally consolidated rather than merged.

ISBN 1-55896-308-1
978-1-55896-308-5
Printed in the USA.
12 11 10 09
10 9 8 7

Howe, Charles A., 1922-
    The larger faith : a short history of American Universalism /
Charles A. Howe.
        p. cm.
    Includes bibliographical references and index.
    ISBN 1-55896-308-1
    1. Universalist churches—United States—History. 2. Universalism—History. 3. United States—Church history.
    I. Title.
BX9933.H69 1992
289. 1'73—dc20   92-44086
                                                                      CIP

Table of Contents

Preface • *ix*

Chapter One • *1*
"Not Hell, But Hope"
John Murray and the Rise of Universalism in
America, 1770–1793

Chapter Two • *17*
"The Doctrine of Atonement Made Rational"
A Transition in Theology and Leadership, 1794–1817

Chapter Three • *33*
"The Prominent Heresy of Our Times"
Hosea Ballou and Universalist Growth, 1818–1845

Chapter Four • *47*
"To Begin a Better State of Things"
Confronting the Problems of the Times, 1846–1869

Chapter Five • *61*
"No Doctrine Not Clearly Taught in the Bible"
The Denomination Grows Conservative, 1870–1892

Chapter Six • *77*
"Improve the Property or Move Off the Premises"
The Struggle Back to Liberalism, 1893–1918

Chapter Seven • *95*
"We Do Not Stand, We Move"
The Search for a New Identity, 1919–1944

Chapter Eight • *111*
"A Circumscribed Universalism Is Unthinkable"
A New Identity Emerging, 1945–1960

Chapter Nine • *127*
"A Bold, Fresh Enterprise of the Liberal Spirit"
Universalism's Contribution to the
Merged Movement, 1961–1993

References • *139*

Appendix • *144*

Selected Bibliography • *146*

Index • *151*

To Russell E. Miller
who supplied most of the materials.

Preface

When Russell Miller was in the final stages of writing *The Larger Hope*, his two-volume history of American Universalism, Alan Seaburg and I were chatting with him about the book at the Harvard Divinity School library. Seaburg suggested that when the project was completed, Miller should then write a short version for the general reader. Miller agreed that this was a good idea but added that if such a book were to be written, it would have to be by somebody else.

Last fall, when I was teaching a survey course in Unitarian Universalist history to students at Wesley Theological Seminary in Washington, DC, I remembered the conversation, realizing that such a short history of Universalism was indeed needed. There were excellent resources available for the class to study—George Huntston Williams's monograph *American Universalism*, David Robinson's *The Unitarians and the Universalists*, Ernest Cassara's documentary history *Universalism in America*, and Miller's history itself—but I found that what was missing was a short chronological history of the American Universalist movement that would provide an overview of the denomination's history and a context and starting point for additional, more detailed study. There was a pressing need, I concluded, for a Universalist counterpart to *A Stream of Light*, the short history of American Unitarianism edited by Conrad Wright and published in connection with the Unitarian denomination's sesquicentennial.

Because the bicentennial of the Universalist denomination's founding was to be celebrated in 1993, the need for such a book became even more urgent. As a result, with the encouragement of Unitarian Universalist Association (UUA) President William Schulz, I began to prepare the short version of Russell Miller's monumental two-volume work that Alan Seaburg had suggested many years ago.

The value of Miller's history has been increasingly appreciated since its publication. An encyclopedic work with literally thousands of references to the original literature, it has stimulated new interest in Universalist historiography by providing a starting place for numerous articles. In recent years it has become apparent that a similar comprehensive study of American Unitarianism is needed as well.

This present volume is almost entirely derivative in its contents: *The Larger Hope* provided most of the factual material and a significant number of the interpretations. Thus, it is gratefully dedicated to Russell Miller, who has expressed deep satisfaction that it has been prepared. I have also found, as did Miller, that Richard Eddy's two-volume *Universalism in America*, published in the 1880s, remains a valuable source of materials, particularly of quotations from original writings. To bring things up-to-date, I have also included material from literature that has appeared since the writing of *The Larger Hope*. Because the contents of this volume are largely derivative, and because it is written chiefly for the general reader, I have not included references to sources in the body of the text. Readers wishing to identify sources can do so by referring to the section on References, which follows Chapter 9.

I have had to omit many important things in preparing a book of this length, and another author would have certainly made different decisions about what to include and what to leave out. Thus, I make no reference to some significant people and events, and I barely mention others. Readers wishing more complete and detailed information should consult the two well-indexed volumes of *The Larger Hope*.

The title of this volume, *The Larger Faith*, is not original. Alan Seaburg had suggested it to Miller for the title of his second volume, Ernest Cassara has used it as the title of the final chapter of his documentary history, and it quite possibly has been used by others in a variety of ways. Still, it seems appropriate here because of how well it captures the all-inclusive vision of modern Universalism.

Unlike Miller, who undertook his work as someone outside the denomination, I was a Universalist before the merger and have been a Unitarian Universalist ever since. While I have made an effort to be objective in my treatment, particularly for the period since the mid-1950s, during which I have been involved in denominational life, some of my prejudices may have unintentionally crept in. To the extent that this has occurred, I apologize.

My appreciation goes out to many people for their help in preparing this book: to UUA President William Schulz for his initial encouragement; to Patricia Frevert, UUA Director of Publications, and Brenda Wong, Project Editor, for guiding the production process through its many stages; to Alan Seaburg, Curator of Manuscripts at the Andover-Harvard Theological Library, Harvard Divinity School, for the original idea and for all his help in locating sources and illustrations; to Charles Gaines, Daniel Hotchkiss, Gordon McKeeman, and Carl Seaburg for reading and criticizing parts of the manuscript; to David Parke for helping me get the project started; to Conrad Wright for making available unpublished material and for advice on several details; to Gladys Harrison for supplying the photograph taken at her late husband's ordination; to Ruth Wallace, Ruby Croom, and Dorothy Chapman for supplying periodicals or information; to the members of the Universalist Bicentennial Committee for their support; to Ernest Cassara, Willard Frank, John Morgan, my wife Ann, and many others for their encouragement; to the students in the Unitarian Universalist history course at Wesley Theological Seminary during the fall semester 1991 for helping me recognize the need for this book; and, most important, to Russell Miller for providing the basic materials from which it has been constructed.

Charles A. Howe
Hyattsville, Maryland
June 1992

Chapter One

"Not Hell, But Hope"

John Murray and the Rise of Universalism in America, 1770–1793

On September 4, 1793, a group of people who called themselves Universalists gathered in the village of Oxford, Massachusetts, for a day of preaching, prayer, fellowship, mutual support, and organizational business. Those present called their meeting a "General Convention" of the "Universal Churches and Societies in Massachusetts, Rhode Island, New Hampshire, Vermont, Connecticut, and New York," and although they could not have known it at the time, their meeting marked the beginning of a new denomination.

No minutes survive from that first meeting—only a circular letter written by the Rev. John Murray, the moderator, on behalf of those attending and addressed to "their brethren in the faith of the gospel . . . and to every church and society scattered abroad" in New England and New York. Nevertheless, the minutes of subsequent meetings seem to indicate that this General Convention was attended by at most a few dozen lay delegates and a handful of ministers. Presumably the worship services and business sessions were held in the new Universalist meeting house which had been erected the previous year. Those delegates who had come from a distance very likely were given overnight home hospitality. One thing is certain. Before adjournment, the delegates made plans for another such meeting to be held the following year. Thus, from an obscure and homely beginning was born an organization that would endure as a separate entity for the next 168 years and that finds embodiment today as an integral part of the Unitarian Universalist Association.

When John Murray arrived in Oxford that September of 1793, it had been exactly twenty-three years since he arrived in the New World, having left England to start a new life for himself after a series of personal tragedies—excommunication from the Methodist Church, the deaths of his son and wife, and a term in debtor's prison. Murray, who had been a lay preacher before his expulsion from the church for his universalist ideas, had become thoroughly disenchanted with institutional religion and had determined never to preach again, but an amazing set of circumstances intervened.

First, the ship on which he had taken passage ran aground on a sandbar off the coast of New Jersey, and Murray went ashore to look for provisions. There he met a farmer named Thomas Potter, an uneducated but deeply religious man who had built a chapel on his property and invited itinerant ministers to preach there, hoping to hear a message that he could wholeheartedly accept. On learning that Murray had once done some preaching, Potter invited him to deliver a sermon the following Sunday. Murray at first refused but gave in to Potter's persistent urging and accepted, provided that the wind did not change first and blow the ship off the sandbar. Potter assured him that it would not, and indeed the wind held steady. Murray's sermon on universal grace, delivered to Potter and his neighbors on September 30, 1770, was evidently exactly the one Potter had long been waiting to hear, and its effect on Murray himself was likewise profound—by the time he had finished, his reservations about preaching were gone forever. Soon after the service was over, a sailor came from the ship with the news that the wind had just changed direction, and the ship was off the sandbar and ready to sail. Potter and Murray both regarded their chance meeting and the postponement of the wind's change as a sign of God's Providence—it was perhaps the only miracle in Universalist history! Murray sailed on to New York City, preached there to an enthusiastic congregation, and was soon traveling up and down the northeastern seaboard, sowing the seeds of Universalism wherever he went.

John Murray was not the first person to preach the Universalist gospel in America. George de Benneville (1703–1793) had come to America from Europe in 1741 to escape persecution, once having almost been beheaded for his universalist convictions. On arriving in America, he settled near Philadelphia, in an area where many of the inhabitants already believed in universal salvation, convinced that a loving God would never condemn any of his children to

Called the "father of Universalism," John Murray
(1741-1815) was minister of the first Universalist
church in America.

eternal damnation. In this congenial atmosphere de Benneville, a physician as well as a preacher, spent most of the rest of his long and useful life. Although he founded no churches in the usual sense, he often preached in informal home settings, advocating a form of universalism that was both mystical and pious. In 1753 he arranged for the publication in America of *The Everlasting Gospel*, written by Georg Klein-Nicolai of Friessdorf under the pseudonym Paul Siegvolck, a book that was to significantly influence Elhanan Winchester, one of the leading proponents of Universalism in the latter part of the century. De Benneville's overall influence on American Universalism, though doubtless significant, is hard to evaluate. It may possibly even have reached Thomas Potter before John Murray's arrival, thus preparing the way for Murray and ultimately for Oxford and the beginnings of a new denomination.

Murray continued preaching throughout New England, New York, and the Middle Atlantic States for several years. Originally he had planned to settle in New Jersey, near the home of his new friend Thomas Potter, but his reputation had spread, and the many invitations he received to preach finally convinced him that the ministry was his true calling. At first he was somewhat less than forthright in his preaching of Universalism, but in time he gained the courage to speak out boldly.

His critics, principally members of the orthodox clergy, were strong in their disapproval. A pamphlet titled "An Attempt to Nip in the Bud the Unscriptural Doctrine of Universal Salvation" described Murray as a "false teacher" of "corrupt tenets." The attempt to discredit the doctrine failed, and Murray continued preaching to large crowds.

He was evidently a powerful, charismatic speaker, with a common touch to which people readily responded. He spoke extemporaneously, and he seems never to have been at a loss for words. Once, when he was preaching in Boston, one of his opponents threw a large rock through the window, narrowly missing his head. Murray promptly picked up the rock and said, "This argument is solid and weighty, but it is neither rational nor convincing." Then, laying the rock aside, he announced, "Not all the stones in Boston, except they stop my breath, shall shut my mouth." On another occasion, his views were challenged by an orthodox minister named Bacon. Murray's response was so warmly applauded by the congregation that some of Bacon's supporters went out, came back with some eggs, and started pelting Murray with them, to which he responded, "These are moving arguments, but I must own at the same time, I have never been so fully treated to Bacon and eggs before in all my life."

More than 200 years later, it is difficult to fully grasp the strong appeal of John Murray's message, but the appeal was certainly there. People migrating from Europe to the New World brought with them religious traditions that included, for the most part, beliefs in hellfire and eternal damnation. Anxiety about one's own fate and that of one's family and friends weighed heavily on many minds, and it was generally conceded that many people were hellbound, whether by God's judgment or exclusion from election. Thus, to hear Murray make a strong case that all were destined to be saved, based on convincing Scriptural arguments, was a welcome and liberating experience. Moreover, at a time when Americans were in the process of attaining political freedom, the prospect of finding religious freedom from dread doctrines was especially attractive.

It is generally conceded that Murray, though a powerful preacher, was not an original thinker. The theology out of which he spoke was essentially that of James Relly, whose preaching and writing had converted Murray to Universalism back in London in the 1750s. Simply stated, Relly's theology, as spelled out in his major book, *Union*, held that Jesus Christ had so thoroughly identified himself with humankind that he became completely tainted with humanity's sins, and that, through his death on the cross, he had atoned for both his own sins and the sins of all humankind, past, present, and future. Relly argued that God the Father could not have possibly forced His Son to die on the cross for sins he had not committed, for that would have been patently unjust. Moreover, even though in the end all humanity would be redeemed through this act of atonement, only true believers in the Christian gospel would, at death, go immediately to heaven; unbelievers would temporarily abide in hell until persuaded to become believers. Relly's (and Murray's) theology was, in essence, a radical form of Calvinism—one in which the concept of the elect was expanded to include all people. Their theology was likewise Trinitarian, at least in the Sabellian sense, where Father, Son, and Holy Spirit were simply different manifestations of the One God rather than three distinct personalities. Many of the fine points of the Rellyan theology were, of course, lost on the majority of Murray's followers—they were simply attracted to the one conclusion that all would be saved.

In December 1774, after four years of itinerant preaching, John Murray decided to make the Massachusetts seaport of Gloucester his home base. He had found a congenial group there, many of whom had already read Relly's *Union* and were sympathetic to its contents. During the Revolutionary War he left briefly to serve as a chaplain in George Washington's Continental Army (Washington supported his appointment in the face of much criticism), but sickness forced him to resign after eight months. Back in Gloucester, he found not only his friends but also a growing number of opponents, who threatened him and tried to force him out of town as a Tory, a British spy, and a vagrant. Murray refused to leave, ignoring an order from the town Committee on Safety that was later upheld by the vote of a town meeting. Then, on January 1, 1779, sixty-one of his followers—thirty-one men and thirty women—organized the Independent Church of Christ, the first Universalist church in America, with Murray as their minister. Many of them had been members of the town's First Parish Church but had left in favor of Murray's hopeful message, which stood in sharp contrast to the grim Calvinistic doctrines they had been hearing. A Universalist meeting house was soon erected, and Murray preached at its dedication on Christmas Day 1780.

As might be expected, the minister and remaining members of the First Parish Church were disturbed by this outbreak of heresy, and they did their best to discredit Murray and his followers. They charged that the Universalists were "but a mere jumble of detached members" rather than a regularly constituted church, and that their presence had kept the community "in one continual hubbub, to the obstructing [of] business, the corrupting of the morals of youth especially, and the total destruction of peace and harmony." In addition, it was pointed out that the Universalists were refusing to pay the tax levied against all residents of the town in support of the established First Parish Church, arguing that they should not be forced to help support a church to which they did not belong and whose doctrines they had rejected. Above all, their minister was accused of being a "false and dangerous man," who, through his pernicious doctrines, was driving Gloucester to the brink of ruin.

In 1782 various articles belonging to members of the Universalist society, including silverware and the anchor of a vessel about to set sail, were confiscated by the authorities and sold at auction to pay the delinquent taxes. The Universalists, despite Murray's reluctance, responded by bringing a lawsuit against First Parish Church, seeking relief from taxes that supported the established church, not only for themselves, but for all religious groups outside the established order. The case dragged on for several years, but in 1786 it was finally decided in favor of the Universalists. From then until 1833, when public support of churches in Massachusetts was discontinued, Universalist churches and others outside the established order received the church taxes paid by their own members. Thus, the Gloucester Universalists struck a major blow for religious freedom and the separation of church and state.

Despite losing the case, the First Parish Church continued its attacks. Since John Murray had never been formally ordained to the ministry, the validity of the marriage ceremonies at which he had officiated was brought into question, and a fine of £50 was levied against him. Refusing to pay, Murray petitioned the state legislature to recognize him as an ordained clergyman by virtue of his eight years of settled ministry to the Gloucester congregation.

Nevertheless, being increasingly uncomfortable with his situation, he thought it wise to leave the country until the matter was decided. In early January 1788, fearing that "prosecutions would be multiplied upon him, by the zeal of his religious adversaries," Murray set sail for England. Back in his native land, from which he had fled in despair eighteen years earlier, he found his preaching warmly received. "Were I an angel descended from above," he said, "I could not be followed with more uniform attention." He was undoubtedly pleased to be described on one occasion as "the most popular preacher in the United States."

By April, having learned that his petition to the legislature had been approved, Murray was on his way back to America, but not without first visiting his aging mother in London. On the return voyage he was invited to preach one Sunday to the passengers and crew. Apparently the crew heard him gladly, but Abigail Adams, who, with her husband, John, was among the passengers, thought his sermon "a sort of familiar talking without any kind of dignity"; she preferred "a discourse that would read well." On Christmas Day, 1788, the Gloucester congregation, taking no chances, renewed Murray's ordination and election as its minister with great fanfare and publicity.

The next few years were probably the happiest of John Murray's life. Not only had his congregation stood solidly behind him while the church tax issue was resolved and his own status affirmed, but a few months after his return from England he had married Judith Sargent Stevens, a thirty-seven-year-old widow from a prominent family, who, with her parents, was a member of the Gloucester congregation. John and Judith had been attracted to each other almost from the start and had carried on a regular correspondence, at the same time observing the proprieties that went with Judith's married state. But after Judith's husband died in the West Indies in 1786, having fled there to escape debtor's prison, a romance quickly blossomed.

Judith Sargent Murray was a remarkable woman, socially ambitious yet at the same time an ardent advocate of women's rights. She was a prolific writer of poetry, drama, and essays, some of them written under pseudonyms to allow her greater freedom of expression. Her essays on the equality of the sexes anticipated most of the arguments put forth by the nascent women's movement a half century later. An energetic, strong-willed woman who wanted not only to be "distinguished and respected" in her lifetime but also to "descend with celebrity into posterity," she would have been pleased to know that she was to find her place in history as America's first leading feminist. Later, after the couple moved to Boston, her personality often caused John problems with the leaders of his congregation, all of them men who were not in the least inclined to welcome input from a woman. Judith remained unintimidated, a thorn in their side to the end, while at the same time strongly encouraging her husband. Clearly, John's success in the ministry was largely due to Judith's unwavering emotional support. The couple had a long and close relationship that ended only with John's death in 1815.

As Universalism spread steadily throughout the Northeast, the First Parish Church in Gloucester complained that it not only had Murray to contend with, but that the town was being "infested" by itinerant Universalist preachers—"strolling mendicants," they were called. While the infestation may have been less severe elsewhere, there were few cities and towns from Portsmouth, New Hamphire, to Philadelphia that had not yet heard the Universalist message. Murray himself had done much to spread the word, but there was an ever-increasing number of those "strolling mendicants" about, preaching the good news that all were destined for salvation. These words of Murray could well have served as their marching orders:

Go out into the highways and byways of America, your new country. Give the people, blanketed with a decaying and crumbling Calvinism, something of your new vision. You may possess only a small light but uncover it, let it shine, use it in order to bring more light and understanding to the hearts and minds of men. Give them, not hell, but hope and courage. Do not push them deeper into their theological despair, but preach the kindness and everlasting love of God.

By 1790 there were at least seventeen Universalist ministers sharing their new vision up and down the seaboard. Many were former Calvinist Baptists; some had been influenced by Murray to change their theology; others had not. Caleb Rich, for example, had come to a Universalist position completely on his own. As a young man, Rich had an intense conversion experience and became a Baptist, but he was troubled by his motive, seeing the fear of hell as an inadequate reason. Later, after a series of dreams and visions, he came to the conviction that all would be saved and that there would be no future punishment (those who died would not be punished for their sins before entering heaven).

Excluded from the Baptist Church for his views, Rich organized a Universalist society in his home town of Warwick, Massachusetts (starting with three members, it grew to ten), and then societies in the nearby towns of Richmond and Jaffrey, across the state line in New Hampshire. Later, the three small groups created a "united" society that met annually to license preachers and ordain ministers. Rich himself was thus ordained and served as minister to the Universalists in all three towns. The Warwick society was actually formed several years before the one in Gloucester, but because of its small size and informal organization it has seldom been recognized as the first Universalist church in America, an honor that has generally been given to the Gloucester congregation. On one occasion Caleb Rich traveled halfway across the state to visit John Murray, who received him cordially, but soon became offended when he realized that Rich's theological views were quite different from his own. Rich returned home "with less reverence for human, and more for divine wisdom."

Like Rich, Elhanan Winchester came to Universalism without Murray's influence. Converted and ordained as a Baptist in 1770, the year of Murray's arrival in the New World, he slowly worked his way to a universalist position with the indirect help of George de Benneville. After being forced out of his church in Philadelphia for his heretical views, Winchester, along with about a hundred of his former Baptist parishioners, began holding services in the original hall of what was to become the University of Pennsylvania. In time this group organized as the Society of Universal Baptists, a flourishing congregation with Winchester as its minister. When Joseph Priestley, the English Unitarian minister and scientist, migrated to America, the Universal Baptists welcomed him to their pulpit. Priestley was, in fact, a universalist as well as a unitarian in his theology. John Murray soon became acquainted with Winchester and realized that he could make a significant contribution to the Universalist cause. "I have a very good opinion of our good Friend Mr. Winchester," he wrote, "and believe he knows a great deal, but not so much of God, or himself as he will know." In 1787 Winchester quite abruptly left his congregation and sailed for England, where he preached for seven years, spawning a small Universalist movement there before returning to America.

Although there were perhaps no more than two dozen organized Universalist societies in existence in 1790, subscribers to the doctrine were found in significant numbers throughout New England, Pennsylvania, and New Jersey. The time seemed ripe to organize. Accordingly, plans were laid for a convention designed to draw together Universalists from "different parts of the continent" to adopt a statement of faith and a plan of government that not only would provide a helpful model for local societies, but also would encourage cooperation between them. As the circular letter promoting the convention put it, the purpose was to unite Universalists "in one General Church in bands of love and uniformity." The first session of the convention was held on May 25, 1790, in the meeting house of Winchester's Society of Universal Baptists in Philadelphia. Seventeen delegates (ten of them ministers) were present: five from Philadelphia, two from other parts of Pennsylvania, eight from New Jersey, one from Virginia, and one—John Murray—from Massachusetts. They represented eight societies, with Murray serving as a delegate from both the Gloucester and Boston churches. The Philadelphia Convention, as it has come to be known, lasted for two full weeks, and the delegates worked their way through an ambitious agenda. By final adjournment they had agreed on Articles of Faith, a Plan of Church Government, and resolutions on "War, Going to Law,

Holding Slaves, Oaths, Submission to Government." Benjamin Rush, a Philadelphia physician, social activist, and signer of the Declaration of Independence, helped organize the convention report into its final form. Though he was never a signed-on member of a Universalist church, Rush was thoroughly universalist in his theology and often attended services at Winchester's church.

The Articles of Faith were as follows:

Sec. 1. Of the Holy Scriptures—We believe the scriptures of the Old and New Testaments to contain a revelation of the perfections and will of God, and the rule of faith and practice.

Sec. 2. Of the Supreme Being—We believe in *One God*, infinite in all his perfections; and that these perfections are all modifications of infinite, adorable, incomprehensible, and unchangeable *Love*.

Sec. 3. Of the Mediator—We believe that there is *One Mediator* between God and man, the man Christ Jesus, in whom dwelleth all the fullness of Godhead bodily; who, by giving himself as a ransom for all, hath redeemed them to God by his blood; and who, by the merit of his death, and the efficacy of his Spirit, will finally restore the whole human race to happiness.

Sec. 4. Of the Holy Ghost—We believe in the *Holy Ghost*, whose office it is to make known to sinners the truth of their salvation, through the medium of the Holy Scriptures, and to reconcile the hearts of the children of men to God, and thereby to dispose them to genuine holiness.

Sec. 5. Of Good Works—We believe in the obligation of the moral law, as the rule of life; and we hold that the love of God manifest to man in a Redeemer, is the best means of producing obedience to that law, and producing a holy, active, and useful life.

These Articles of Faith were, of necessity, written in quite general terms because of the theological differences among the delegates. Most of those present were former Calvinist Baptists who had simply modified their theology to include all people within the elect; Murray, of course, was a Rellyan, the only one in attendance; and the delegates from Philadelphia had doubtless absorbed much of Winchester's unique theology. The one basic belief shared by those present was the conviction that all people would eventually, after death, be restored to happiness.

The Plan of Church Government adopted by the delegates was described as "nearly that of the Congregational Church," with sections on the church, the call and ordination of officers (bishops and deacons—the terms bishop, elder, minister, pastor, and teacher were considered synonymous), worship, ordinances, membership, marriage, the instruction of children (it was recommended that each church have a school at which reading, writing, arithmetic, and psalmody were taught—free to children of the poor—all this "as a necessary introduction to the knowledge of the gospel"), and "the communion of the churches" (this through annual conventions at which "messengers" would report on behalf of their churches and plans would be made for propagating the faith). Given the diversity of views of the delegates (a characteristic of Universalism from the beginning), no part of this plan was binding—these were simply recommendations to the churches. For instance, Murray opposed baptism while the former Baptists continued to favor it. He devised in its place a ceremony of child dedication that was in form, if not in substance, much like those used in Unitarian Universalist churches today.

Of the resolutions adopted by the convention (these, too, were recommendations), the one on slavery is of particular importance because it applied the basic Universalist belief in the ultimate worth of every human being to one of the pressing social problems of the times. "We believe it to be inconsistent with the union of the human race . . . to hold any part of our fellow-creatures in bondage," said the resolution. "We therefore recommend a total refraining from the African trade, and the adoption of prudent measures for the gradual abolition of the slavery of the negroes in our country, and for the instruction and education of their children . . ."

The Philadelphia Convention of 1790 represented a productive and promising first step toward denominational organization, and before adjournment the delegates voted to reconvene the following May. Annual conventions continued through 1809, until it became apparent that Philadelphia was too far from the center of Universalist activity to serve as the site for national meetings. When the New England Universalists had gathered "in General Convention" at Oxford, Massachusetts, in 1793, their meeting was considered to be of secondary importance. In fact, the New England Universalists had felt it necessary to get permission from the Philadelphia Convention to hold their own meeting, pointing out that the distance to Philadelphia was so great that very few of them could ever attend the convention there. Indeed, except for the occasional attendance of Murray, New England was never represented in Philadelphia at all. Within a decade, however, with the rapid growth of Universalism in New England, the convention organized at Oxford became the more prominent of the two, in time evolving into the General Convention for the denomination as a whole.

With the further passage of time, the General Convention became the Universalist Church of America, which, in 1961, merged with the American Unitarian Association to form the Unitarian Universalist Association. Thus, 1993 became the bicentennial year for the senior partner of the merged movements.

Murray's trip to Philadelphia in 1790 was a stimulating one. In addition to attending the convention, he met Benjamin Rush, received favorable attention from Benjamin Franklin's family, preached several times to large congregations, and was approached by members of the Society of Universal Baptists about becoming their minister (Elhanan Winchester had gone to England three years earlier). In New York, on the trip back to Boston, he and Judith visited Vice President and Mrs. Adams and President Washington, presenting the President with a congratulatory message from the convention on his election to office. The disheartened immigrant had come a long way since landing on the Jersey coast twenty years before!

Moving on to Connecticut, Murray found himself in great demand as a preacher. "There from my first entrance into the State," he wrote a friend, "in every town the meeting-houses were opened to receive me, and many faithful souls I met, where I did not expect to meet any. Surely this is the Lord's doing, and it is marvellous in our eyes." Being warmly received was nothing new to Murray, of course, but being a man who delighted in occupying the center of attention, he obviously relished it. During his time in Connecticut, however, he found some unsettling developments in some parts of the state. He wrote, "I found much to trouble me, not from my enemies, but from my friends. There are some dangerous errors creeping in among the people, and I am afraid they will prevail. They teach that the day of the Lord is past, that there is no future sorrow to be apprehended, that there is no devil but in the imagination. . . ." Murray went on to say that he wished to see more churches established in order that correct doctrine might be taught more clearly. "Those who hold these wild notions are not fond of church fellowship, they are fond of liberty in its wildest latitude."

Perhaps as a direct result of his Connecticut experience, Murray published in 1791 a lengthy pamphlet titled "Some Hints Relative to the Forming of a Christian Church." In it, after briefly describing the duties of a Christian citizen, a plan of church organization, and his ideas regarding scripture and ordinances, he identified seven systems of doctrine considered "Universalist" by their adherents that were in error. Most of the theological fine points of Murray's analysis are difficult for the modern reader to follow, but among the errors he was addressing were the beliefs that "no future sorrow is to be apprehended" and "that there is no Devil but in the imagination." Some of Elhanan Winchester's doctrines also disturbed Murray, especially since they were gaining acceptance even though Winchester himself remained in England. Murray particularly objected to the belief that "all who are not . . . pure in heart, must, before they see God in glory, pass through a purgatorial fire, and there suffer some thousands of years, until they have paid the utmost farthing of the debt they owed"—all this despite the fact that Christ had already paid their debt. Another group's deficiency in belief is easily grasped—its members, "as the manner of some was in the apostolic age, forsake the assembling of themselves together."

However obscure some of Murray's distinctions may appear, it is evident that he was deeply concerned that much unsound doctrine was being preached under the Universalist name, and that he was writing to counteract the tendency he saw in others to reject the pure Rellyan system. He had no way of knowing it at the time, but greater departures from Relly's theology lay ahead. In that same year, a twenty-year-old farm lad in New Hampshire named Hosea Ballou was making his first stumbling efforts at preaching.

Despite Murray's anxiety, his wish for more churches was being fulfilled. At the 1792 Philadelphia Convention it was reported that forty societies were in existence, a significant increase in just two years. Moreover, some societies were experiencing significant growth, among them the Universal Society in Boston, organized in 1785 with Murray's help and ably led by George Richards, a schoolmaster and part-time preacher. Murray preached there occasionally, but in 1792, "such was the increasing interest in Boston that Mr. Murray yielded to the solicitations of his friends there, and gave one-half of his time to the supply of their pulpit." Within a year, he had accepted a call to become the society's full-time minister with the understanding that he would "preach in Boston every Sabbath, except what time *he* may judge necessary to visit our friends in Gloucester." A few weeks after the Oxford Convention, on October 24, 1793, he became the society's "pastor and teacher."

The installation itself was a grand success. The service was led by Deacon Oliver Lane, who called on "the people usually worshipping in this place" to show whether they wanted to install Murray as their minister "by the usual sign of uplifted hands." Murray received a unanimous vote, then reaffirmed his "willingness to be acknowledged as their pastor and teacher," at which time Lane declared him installed. According to the record, "Mr. Murray's reply was animated & replete with affection." After a sermon by Murray, "the whole was concluded by an anthem adapted to the occasion; with a decorum which gave satisfaction to a *numerous, respectable,* and *attentive audience.*" John Murray's new ministry appeared to be off to a good start.

Murray's coming to Boston could certainly be considered a move upward. The newer Boston society may have had slightly fewer members at the time than Gloucester (eighty-two proprietors or pew holders, compared with eighty-seven), but it appeared to be a more dynamic congregation with a far greater potential for growth. Then, too, the salary was double that in Gloucester (£4 per Sabbath, compared with £2), but this was doubtless more important to Judith Murray than to John, who seemed quite unconcerned about money. ("The preacher," Judith once wrote, "was accustomed to withdraw from the approaches of affluence.") Most important, though, the move to Boston gave Murray, generally acknowledged as Universalism's leading spokesperson, the opportunity to be heard in the cultural and religious center of New England, if not America. As 1793 ended, the prospects for Universalism in general and for John Murray in particular had never seemed brighter.

Chapter Two

"The Doctrine of Atonement Made Rational"

A Transition in Theology and Leadership, 1794–1817

In September 1794, when Universalists from New England and New York State again convened in Oxford, John Murray did not attend. As the minutes of the Boston proprietors explain, it was "voted, that Mr. Elhanan Winchester be requested to attend as a Delegate in Behalf of this Society, in Room of Mr. Murray who was Chosen for that Purpose, but whose present Indisposition prevents his Attendance."

Despite Murray's absence, the convention, with Winchester serving as moderator, was a great success, with a higher attendance and more localities represented than the year before. Among their other actions, the delegates "chose a committee to compose a short piece, simplifying a system of religion adapted to the capacity of children," "adopted the Philadelphia platform of articles of faith and form of church government," and "chose Elders Michael Coffin and Joab Young missionaries, to go forth in a circuitous manner and preach the everlasting gospel. . . ." The two new missionaries were appointed to supplement the work of Murray and Winchester, who had been traveling throughout New England as time permitted, as had the young lay preacher, Hosea Ballou. The high point of the convention came when Ballou found himself ordained in a most unusual way. Winchester, on reaching the climax of his sermon at the concluding service, suddenly pressed a Bible against the surprised Ballou's chest and ordered him charged on the spot! (Later, in 1803, to make sure that the legality of the weddings at which he officiated would not be challenged, as were some of the weddings performed by Murray, Ballou was reordained by the New England Convention in a more formal manner.) Once ordained, Ballou rose steadily toward a position of leadership. At the 1795 convention he was chosen as clerk, Murray as moderator; at the 1799 convention, Ballou himself was moderator.

Hosea Ballou was a creative, original thinker, influenced by the writings of deistic rationalists like Ethan Allen and Thomas Paine, yet thoroughly committed to the authority of the Bible as the source of revelation. By 1795, a year after his ordination, he had reasoned his way to a unitarian position with regard to the nature of Christ and to the beginnings of a radically new understanding of atonement—one that held that it is humanity that needs to be reconciled to God, not the other way around. He had also become a powerful, persuasive preacher, and his views not only began to gain wide acceptance within the Universalist ranks but also to inspire many to join those ranks.

Quite predictably, John Murray was upset by those views, but nevertheless, in the fall of 1798 he invited Ballou to fill his Boston pulpit while he was "going for a few weeks to the southward." Things went well enough until Ballou's last sermon, when Judith Murray became so upset that she had the following announcement read from the choir loft: "I wish to give notice that the doctrine which has been preached here this afternoon is not the doctrine which is usually preached in this house." Ballou simply remarked, "The audience will please to take notice of what our brother has said," and then announced the closing hymn. Many members of the society, some of whom had urged Murray to invite Ballou in the first place, were deeply embarrassed by what had happened and apologized to Ballou after the service, but the relationship between John Murray and Ballou, already tenuous, presumably was not helped by the incident. Murray must have sometimes regretted that Winchester, rather than he, had represented the Boston society at the 1794 convention, since Winchester's impromptu act of ordination there had helped propel Ballou into prominence.

Murray's trip "to the southward" had its compensations, however. In Philadelphia, which had replaced New York as the nation's capital, he renewed his friendship with John Adams, the new president, dining with him often and meeting the leaders of government. Adams flattered Murray by claiming that Murray had

The leading theologian and "elder statesman" of Universalism, Hosea Ballou (1772-1852) once traveled the country as a circuit preacher, spreading the Universalist gospel.

performed "a great feat—next to a miracle" by enticing Vice President Thomas Jefferson to come to church to hear him preach. Meanwhile, the growth of Universalism continued. By the end of the century there were roughly three dozen ministers preaching the gospel of universal salvation up and down the Atlantic seaboard, from the District of Maine to the Commonwealth of Virginia. According to Richard Eddy, the nineteenth-century historian, "Everywhere the people were eager to hear; and devoted, saintly men were at great personal sacrifice going forth, at the call of God, to occupy the opening fields." By 1801 Universalism was being preached in Georgia; by 1803 the first society in upstate New York had been established at Hartwick, near Cooperstown.

In that same year, the New England Convention, as the annual assembly had come to be called, met in the village of Winchester, New Hampshire, with thirty-eight societies represented. There, in addition to granting letters of fellowship to Abner Kneeland and Nathaniel Stacy, men who would later make their mark on the denomination, the delegates adopted a Plan of General Association and a Profession of Belief that would serve the denomination for the rest of the century. The New England Convention had quickly adopted the Articles of Faith and Plan of Church Government passed by the Philadelphia Convention in 1790, but over the years there had been changes in both theological emphasis and polity. In addition, the delegates felt the need to establish firmly the validity of ordinations of Convention ministers. For these reasons, a committee had been appointed to formulate more adequate statements, and its report, presented to the delegates at Winchester, served as the basis for the new Profession of Belief and Plan of Church Government.

The Profession of Belief adopted by the delegates (later to be known as the Winchester Profession) was both broad and brief, consisting of but three articles:

Article the First. We believe that the Holy Scriptures of the Old and New Testaments contain a revelation of the character of God, and of the duty, interest and final destination of mankind.

Article the Second. We believe that there is one God, whose nature is Love, revealed in one Lord Jesus Christ, by one Holy Spirit of Grace, who will finally restore the whole family of mankind to holiness and happiness.

Article the Third. We believe that holiness and true happiness are inseparably connected, and that believers ought to be careful to maintain order, and practice good works; for these things are good and profitable to men.

These three articles are similar in content to those on the Holy Scriptures, the Supreme Being, and Good Works adopted thirteen years earlier at Philadelphia, but this time no articles on the Mediator and the Holy Ghost were included, possibly because of the influence of Ballou's rational Unitarian theology. Moreover, the following was appended to the Profession:

> Yet while we . . . adopt a general *Profession of Belief* . . . we leave it to the several Churches and Societies, or to smaller associations of churches . . . to continue or adopt within themselves, such more particular articles of faith . . . as may appear to them best under their particular circumstances, provided they do not disagree with our general *Profession.* . . .

Although this statement, which became known as the Liberty Clause, has often been invoked in defense of freedom of conscience, the liberty of belief that it guaranteed was somewhat limited, as the final phrase makes clear.

Debate preceding adoption of the Profession was heated. Stacy later wrote that it was "probably the longest and warmest . . . that had ever been known in that deliberative body." Another minister compared the proposed statement to a calf: "It is harmless now . . . (but) its horns will grow, and then it will begin to hook." In the end, after some of the more vocal opponents had left for home, the Profession, in the interest of harmony, was unanimously approved. In a relatively short time the Winchester Profession became the generally accepted standard of belief for the Universalist denomination as a whole, and remained so until it was supplemented by a new statement ninety-six years later.

The Plan of General Association was also adopted unanimously, with considerably less debate. It formalized in some detail the convention's practices that were already in effect for the granting of fellowship to societies and ministers; the ordination and discipline of ministers; and the conduct of convention business. It is worth noting that John Murray, whose health had begun to fail, was not among the eighteen ministers present; nor was Elhanan Winchester, who had died some years before. As might be expected, Hosea Ballou was on hand, taking an active part in the proceedings as the newly called minister of the united societies of Barnard, Woodstock, Hartland, and Bethel, Vermont. The shift in leadership was well under way.

Except for the congregations in Boston, Portsmouth, and New Haven, the societies represented at the 1803 General Convention were located in small New England villages—places like Charlton, Goshen, Hinesburg, Benson, and North Henniker. Ministers usually served several of these small societies, and many also farmed or taught school to eke out a living.

There was a strong missionary spirit among them, well exemplified by Nathaniel Stacy, who in 1805 began to carry the Universalist message westward into the heart of New York State. Born of Universalist parents in Gloucester, Stacy had been encouraged to enter the ministry by Ballou, who served for a short time as his mentor. In those days, a man wanting to enter the Universalist ministry first had to find an experienced minister willing to take him under his wing and teach him theology and homiletics. Once the apprentice was judged ready, he went to the Convention to seek fellowship and then ordination. Stacy, who had received fellowship in 1803, was ordained in 1805, just before setting out for New York State. The following April, he helped organize the Western Association of Universalists in the State of New York, with delegates from all three societies in the area attending the first meeting and Ballou himself on hand to bless the occasion. The meeting was held in Chenango County, in the ballroom of a newly erected tavern. At the Association's meeting a year later, Stacy reported that he had preached in the towns of "Paris, Bridgewater, Deerfield, Litchfield, Westmoreland, Rome, Western, Floyd, Eaton, and Norwich, besides the villages of Utica, Whitesboro and Clinton; and various other neighborhoods in the towns of Hamilton, Madison and Sangerfield." He also reported having organized societies in the towns of Madison, Eaton, and Western. A frail, sickly man, small in stature, Stacy was nevertheless an indefatigable missionary in the Universalist cause, preaching wherever he could get "ten or a dozen willing to listen to [his] message," whether in a meetinghouse, tavern, hay barn, or grove.

Like Ballou, Stacy was a skillful debater, and sermon "talk-backs" were a routine part of his services. "My general practice," he wrote, "was, to give liberty for remarks, or questions, at the close of the discourse, and wait a reasonable time for those who wished to speak, before dismissing the congregation."

Itinerant preaching was a hard way to make a living. "The people," he was to write later, "considered that they were doing the preacher overmuch honor, and quite as much as they could afford to do, to spend time to give him a hearing, without once thinking he needed anything else. Sometimes we were obliged to ride whole days without money enough in our pockets to buy a meal of victuals, or a mess of oats for our horses, and even be compelled to pawn our pocket knives to get through the turnpike toll gate to go to the place of appointment, and then take a circuitous route back to avoid the gate, so as to get home again, because we did not get enough for our services to pay the toll. . . . But some one had to do it, or else there would be no Universalist societies or congregations. . . . All this we did; and all this was necessary to be done, in order to clear the ground, and plant the seed, which has now come up, and is producing a luxuriant crop."

Stacy pursued his missionary work in New York State for twenty-five years, then continued it in Pennsylvania and Michigan. At the end of his autobiography, he provided the following statistics: "I have preached more or less in ten states of the Union; have delivered up to the present time, December 31, 1848, four thousand seven hundred and forty-nine discourses, which I have minutes of, and many of which I have kept no minutes; I have officiated at three hundred and sixty-eight funerals, and solemnized two hundred and twenty-eight marriages." Stacy died in 1868, in his ninetieth year.

The first Universalist woman to brave public opinion and preach her faith was Maria Cook, who delivered a sermon to a meeting of the Western Association in Bainbridge, New York, in 1811. Some of the delegates "were a little fastidious about allowing a woman to preach, supposing St. Paul forbade it," but since "the phenomenon of a female preacher . . . was so *extraordinary* and curiosity was on tiptoe among the mass of the congregation," the objections were at last withdrawn. It was reported that "there was not a sermon delivered with more eloquence, more correctness of diction, or pathos, or one listened to with more devout attention . . . as the one she delivered." Afterward, Cook received an informal letter of

fellowship that she modestly accepted, only to destroy it a few
weeks later because, on reflection, she decided that it was "an
insincere token of fellowship."
For a while Cook received many invitations to preach, but
eventually those who thought sermons by women inappropriate
began to voice their opposition. Hurt by this criticism, she began to
spend more and more time defending her right to preach, and as
she did, her sermons became less interesting. Her popularity
waned, and eventually she gave up preaching altogether. Maria
Cook had, however, clearly demonstrated that women could preach,
and preach effectively. It was to be another half century before
women began to be accepted in Universalist pulpits.
In 1805 Hosea Ballou published *A Treatise on Atonement* "in
which," according to the title page, "the finite nature of sin is
argued, its cause and consequences as such; the necessity and
nature of Atonement; and its glorious consequences, in the final
reconciliation of all men to holiness and happiness." It was an
octavo volume of 216 pages, printed in Randolph, Vermont, and it
made an immediate and lasting impact. Over time it has gone
through sixteen editions, the most recent in 1986. In it, Ballou
developed the innovative theological views that he had begun to
preach a decade earlier and that had so distressed the Murrays.
Ballou divided his treatise into three parts, the first on "Sin,"
the second on "the Atonement for Sin," the third on "the
Consequences of Atonement for Mankind." The style, with its
complicated sentence structures and old-fashioned vocabulary, is
difficult for most modern readers, and it takes concentration and
effort to follow many of Ballou's arguments. On close analysis,
however, the main points become clear, and the reader cannot help
but be impressed by the author's coherent, closely reasoned
presentation. Because of the great significance of the *Treatise* as
the most original and influential statement of nineteenth-century
Universalist theology, it is worth discussing in some detail.
Ballou begins it by defining sin as "the violation of a law which
exists in the mind, which law is the imperfect knowledge men have
of moral good." In stating this, he concedes that human beings can
never fully grasp the nature of moral good; the most they can do is
come to the best understanding of it that is possible for them. "This
law is transgressed, whenever, by the influence of temptation, a
good understanding yields to a contrary choice." In short, to sin is
to act in a way at variance with that dictated by the best human

understanding of what is morally good.

He then makes a point fundamental to the treatise's whole argument: "Sin, in its nature, ought to be considered finite and limited, rather than infinite and unlimited, as has, by many been supposed." (He points out later that many have concluded that sin is infinite and unlimited because, according to their erroneous understanding of atonement and deity, it was necessary for God himself, the infinite and unlimited one, to atone for humanity's sin by his death on the cross; in this view, nothing less would have been sufficient.)

As Ernest Cassara explains, Ballou's argument is this: "If the usual theory (i.e., that sin is infinite) is true, the interesting situation occurs of finite man thwarting the law of an infinite legislator, God. 'With eyes open, the reader cannot but see, that if sin is infinite because it is committed against an infinite law, whose author is God, the design of Deity must be *abortive.* . . .' " Given Ballou's definition of sin as dependent on an imperfect human understanding of moral good, it would never warrant infinite and unlimited punishment from a loving and just God. "All our knowledge of moral holiness," he adds by way of explanation, "is but a faint resemblance of that sublime rectitude from which the most upright of the sons of men are at great distance."

God, argues Ballou, is in a sense "the author of sin," since, being almighty, God would not allow it to exist unless it served some useful purpose. "Man's main object," he writes, "in all he does, is happiness. . . . What would induce men to form societies; to be at the expense of supporting governments; to acquire knowledge; to learn the sciences, or till the earth, if they believed they could be as happy without as with?" (Modern readers might well substitute "fulfillment" for "happiness" here.) The problem, then, is deciding what actions do in fact lead to true happiness rather than to sinfulness. Sin, Ballou maintains, is the fruit of the flesh, as opposed to the spirit. He cites St. Paul, who identified the works of the flesh as "adultery, fornication, uncleanness, lasciviousness, idolatry, witchcraft, hatred, variance, emulation, wrath, strife, seditions, heresies, envying, murders, drunkenness, revellings, and such like"—all of which are practiced by men and women in misguided searches for happiness.

In the second part of his treatise Ballou describes erroneous theories of atonement, in which he openly ridicules the doctrine of the Trinity. These erroneous theories, he writes, "all contend that the Mediator is really God; that the Godhead consists of three distinct persons, viz., Father, Son, and Holy Ghost; that these three distinct persons are equal in power and glory, and eternally and essentially one. . . . I contend that if (the Mediator) be the Son of God, he is the Son of himself, and is his own father; that he is no more the Son of God than God is his son! To say of two persons, exactly of the same age, that one of them is a real son of the other, is to confound good sense. . . . If the Godhead consists of three distinct persons, and each of these persons be infinite, the whole Godhead amounts to the amazing sum of infinity multiplied by three! If it is said that neither of these three persons alone is infinite, I say the three together, with the addition of a million more such, would not make an infinite being." Ballou goes on to affirm the Unitarian (or Arian) position that Christ is not part of the Godhead but rather a lesser created being. (Interestingly, Ballou seldom attacked the doctrine of the Trinity in his sermons, quite possibly because his audiences were not interested in such an abstract subject and such attacks were not essential to the points he was making; outspoken as he was, his avoidance of the subject was certainly not due to timidity.)

Ballou then goes on to develop his own doctrine of atonement, asserting that "atonement signifies reconciliation, or satisfaction, which is the same. It is a being unreconciled to truth and justice which needs reconciliation; and it is a dissatisfied being which needs satisfaction. Therefore I raise my inquiry on the question, Is God the unreconciled or dissatisfied party, or is man?" Citing the story of the Garden of Eden, from which came the Calvinist notion of original sin, Ballou claims that Adam, not God, is clearly the unreconciled party—"he believed God to be his enemy, in consequences of his disobedience." God, on the other hand, was not unreconciled to Adam—"God's calling Adam, in the cool of the day, and asking him where he was, clothing him with garments of skins, and promising that the seed of woman should bruise the serpent's head, are beautiful representations of the parental love and fatherly care of the Creator. . . . To say that God loved man any less after transgression than before, denies his unchangeability; but to say that man was wanting in love to God, places him in his real character. As God was not the unreconciled party, no atonement was necessary for his reconciliation." Rather, man was the unreconciled party, and "the atonement was necessary to renew his love to his Creator."

Ballou then demonstrates "that the atonement by Christ was the effect and not the cause of God's love to man. . . . The [contrary] belief that the great Jehovah was offended by his creatures to that degree, that nothing but the death of Christ, or the endless misery of mankind, could appease his anger, is an idea that has done more injury to the Christian religion than the writings of all its opposers, for many centuries. The error has been fatal to the life and spirit of the religion of Christ in our world . . ." Rather than coming to appease God's anger, Christ came to the world to demonstrate the power of the law of love through which men and women can turn away from sin and be reconciled to God.

As for the meaning of the crucifixion, Ballou has this to say: "The literal death of the man, Christ Jesus, is figurative. . . . The literal body of Jesus represented the whole letter of the law. . . . The death of the body of Jesus represented the death and destruction of the letter, when the spirit comes forth, bursting the veil thereof, which is represented by the resurrection of Jesus from the dead."

The fruit of the spirit is love, which will guide men and women to choose that which is morally good. "Atonement by Christ was never intended to perform impossibilities," Ballou continues, "therefore it was never designed to make men agree and live in peace while they are destitute of love one to another; but it is calculated and designed to inspire the mind with that true love which will produce peace in Jesus. . . . Atoning grace produces all which the Bible means by conversion, or being born of the Spirit." Nor is this atoning love reserved for Christians. Ballou makes explicit his conviction that "this love, which is the spirit of the life of Jesus Christ" is not confined "particularly to names, sects, denominations, people, or kingdoms."

In part three of the treatise Ballou contends that "the consequence of atonement is the universal holiness and happiness of mankind." After refuting in detail the arguments raised against the doctrine of universal salvation, he builds his case for the doctrine on the following grounds: First, the nature of divine goodness dictates that God would not "create a being that would experience more misery than happiness"; second, "if God be infinitely good . . . then all beings whom his power produced are the objects of his goodness"; third, since God is infinite in power, he created all things; and fourth, "if the Almighty . . . did not possess power sufficient to make all his creatures happy it was not an act of goodness in him to create them." In short, universal reconciliation

is the product of the all-powerful, all-loving nature of God. The
process of reconciliation may admittedly be slow in many cases. In
fact, Ballou is forced to conclude that, since "many are going out of
this world daily in a state of sinfulness and unreconciliation to
God," there may be an "alteration in the soul for the better after it
leaves this natural life." Ballou would later change his view on
this, precipitating a heated controversy when he did.

Near the end of his treatise, Ballou pleads with his fellow
Universalists for tolerance and open-mindedness. "Be cautious of
any system of divinity," he warns. "The moment we fancy ourselves
infallible, every one must come to our peculiarities or we cast them
away. Even the truth may be held in unrighteousness. . . . The
cause of truth wants nothing in its service but the fruits of the
Spirit, which are love, joy, peace, gentleness, goodness, faith,
meekness and temperance. . . . Attend to the exhortation, 'Let
brotherly love continue.' If we agree in brotherly love, there is no
disagreement that can do us any injury, but if we do not, no other
agreement can do us any good. . . . Let us endeavor to 'keep the
unity of the Spirit in the bond of peace.' "

Ballou ends the treatise by "humbly hoping and expecting the
glorious increase and extensive growth of what I have (though
feebly) contended for; namely, the holiness and happiness of all
mankind. I look with strong expectation to that period when all sin
and every degree of unreconciliation will be destroyed by the
divine power of that love which is stronger than death. . . . Then
shall the great object of the Saviour's mission be accomplished. . . .
The Son shall deliver up the kingdom to God the Father; the
eternal radiance shall shine, and God shall be all in all."

A Treatise on Atonement, written by a young, largely self-taught
country preacher, is a remarkable document that stood as the
major statement of Universalist theology for at least a century.

In the summer of 1809, Hosea Ballou, his reputation by now
well established, received an invitation from the Universalist society
in Portsmouth to become its minister. It was a tempting offer. Not
only was the salary much higher than the one he was receiving
from the united societies in Vermont (there were now five of them),
but Portsmouth, as the largest town in New Hampshire and an
important seaport and commercial center, would offer him a much
larger audience. He had served the Vermont societies for almost
seven years, and the relationship had been a good one, but he was
thirty-eight years old, married, and had a growing family. After

discussing the matter with his Vermont parishioners and receiving their blessing to move on, Ballou accepted the offer. That fall he and his family moved to Portsmouth.

The Portsmouth ministry was quite different from his circuit-riding ministry in Vermont. With but a single congregation to serve (a relatively rare situation for a Universalist minister in those days), Ballou found himself with new parish responsibilities—a more intense relationship with his parishioners, the religious education of children (there were no Sunday schools in those days, but Ballou prepared a catechism for parents to teach in their homes), and a heavier load of sermon preparation (he now was preaching two or three times each Sunday from the same pulpit). One of the important compensations for his new settlement was the collegial relationship he developed with three neighboring ministers who were also serving large parishes—Edward Turner of Salem, Massachusetts, Thomas Jones of Gloucester, and Abner Kneeland of Charlestown, Massachusetts. The four men formed a support and study group called the Gloucester Conference, which met regularly to share and discuss papers on assigned subjects.

All in all, despite some controversies with orthodox ministers, Ballou's first three years at Portsmouth went smoothly, with large congregations turning out to hear him preach. In 1812, however, controversy erupted within the parish itself.

The war with England had begun, and President Madison called for a national day of prayer in support of the war. Ballou, who seldom spoke on political matters from the pulpit, nevertheless answered Madison's call with a strong sermon in support of the president's policies. While the majority of the congregation agreed with their minister, the wealthy shipowners in the church, whose businesses had been badly hurt by the war, strongly objected and in time withdrew their support. As a result, the church's financial position became so weakened that Ballou was forced to open a private school to provide his family with a second income.

He recruited his grandnephew and namesake, Hosea Ballou 2nd, to help him in this enterprise, and before long the younger Ballou, then seventeen, was not only teaching in the school but also preparing for the ministry under his granduncle's guidance. Thus began a long and fruitful relationship between the two, and the younger Ballou went on to a distinguished career as minister, editor, and educator.

The situation in the church remained difficult, however, and when, early in 1815, the elder Ballou received a call from the Salem congregation, he accepted it. He was to remain in Salem for only two-and-a-half years, when events dictated a move to Boston, where he would help establish a new Universalist society.

At the time Ballou moved to Salem, John Murray's health was extremely precarious. His Boston ministry, after its promising start in 1793, had not proved a happy one. As early as 1801, he confided to a colleague that he was sorry he had ever left Gloucester. Murray found the proprietors of the Boston church difficult to get along with and determined to maintain control. Early in his ministry, the members of the Standing Committee had dunned him when he was late in paying his pew tax, and they had required him to get permission before making pulpit announcements. After the onset in 1801 of the "paralitic disorder" that was to undermine his health, Murray found himself repeatedly at odds with the proprietors over salary, leaves of absence for health reasons, and arrangements for supplying the pulpit in his absence. There even was an ongoing squabble over who would pay for Murray's firewood! The relationship between minister and congregation was not helped by his wife Judith, who outspokenly took her husband's part.

In 1809 Murray suffered a severe stroke, which left him incapacitated for the rest of his life. After that, on the few occasions when he preached, he had to be carried to the pulpit in an armchair. It was soon obvious that, although Murray would continue as senior minister, the society needed another minister to carry on its work. Edward Mitchell, who shared Murray's theology, was persuaded to move from New York City, but after a promising start, he left Boston abruptly, never giving an adequate explanation for his action. In time, Paul Dean, a young, handsome, articulate minister, was recruited from upstate New York as Murray's associate. Dean would stay with the church for a decade, but his ministry was marked by controversy over his theology, which was not Rellyan, and his personality, which was both petulant and manipulative.

In his last years the bedridden John Murray felt increasingly abandoned by his church and rejected by his colleagues. When he died in September 1815, Edward Mitchell was the only Universalist minister who shared his theological position. His funeral, however, was well attended by both parishioners and colleagues, Hosea Ballou among them. After the funeral, Judith presented the Standing Committee with a bill for the new clothes she had bought for the occasion, but since the purchase had not been authorized, the Committee refused to pay. Judith Murray spent her last years living with her daughter in Mississippi, where she completed her husband's half-finished autobiography and edited for publication three volumes of his letters and sermon notes. Although John Murray's body outlived his theology and his influence, we do well to remember that it was he, far more than any other person, who made Universalism a significant force in American religious life, and thus, he properly deserves to be called "the Father of American Universalism."

In the years preceding Murray's death, Hosea Ballou had repeatedly been urged to move to Boston and lead a Universalist society there. He had always rejected these overtures, recognizing that such a move would certainly threaten John Murray and undermine his ministry. But after Murray's death, Ballou felt free to entertain such an invitation. He did not have to wait long. In December 1816 a group of his admirers, including a few former leaders of the First Universal Society, organized the Second Society of Universalists in the Town of Boston and erected a building that was dedicated the following October. Paul Dean, who had remained at the First Universal Society after Murray's death, sat in the pulpit with the other participants at the dedication service but declined to take part, claiming he was feeling ill; it was clear that he was not enthusiastic about the new society. When the Second Society's members voted unanimously to call Ballou as their minister, he promptly accepted and was installed on Christmas Day, 1817, by which time Dean had recovered sufficiently to deliver the installation sermon. (Early Universalists regarded Christmas Day as an ideal time for celebrating special occasions. The Gloucester meeting house had been dedicated on Christmas Day, 1780; the Boston Universalists had purchased their first meeting house on Christmas Day, 1785; and the Gloucester congregation, with great fanfare, had celebrated Murray's reordination on Christmas Day, 1788.)

By coming to Boston, the leading city of New England, Ballou had firmly established himself as the spokesperson for the growing Universalist denomination. The number of societies and ministers in fellowship with the New England Convention was continuing to increase, great activity was reported as far south as Philadelphia, rapid growth was taking place in western New York State, and the first Universalist society had been organized in Ohio. Ballou himself was preaching an aggressive Universalism three times every Sunday to full houses, and visitors to Boston who heard him were taking the Universalist message back home with them to spawn new societies. The denomination seemed on the verge of an explosive growth.

Chapter Three

"The Prominent Heresy of Our Times"

Hosea Ballou and Universalist Growth, 1818–1845

Hosea Ballou would serve the Second Society in Boston for twenty-eight years, until his retirement from the active ministry in 1845. It was a time of great vitality and growth for the Universalist movement, one which Richard Eddy, writing in the 1880s, termed the most active and aggressive period of all. Ballou himself played a major role in what took place, not only through the power of his preaching and the attractiveness of his theology, but also through his active role in denominational meetings, his journalistic endeavors, and his teaching of would-be ministers.

During this period, the movement continued to spread westward and southward through the efforts of itinerant preachers like Stephen R. Smith in upstate New York, Nathaniel Stacy in New York, Pennsylvania, and Michigan, and George Rogers, a lay preacher who, from 1829 until his death in 1846, traveled tirelessly throughout the Southeast and the border states of the Midwest. At the same time substantial growth was taking place in most of New England. By 1845 state conventions had been organized in all the New England States, New York, Ohio, Illinois, Michigan, Iowa, Pennsylvania, New Jersey, South Carolina, and Georgia, as well as a Southern Convention, which included Maryland, Virginia, and North Carolina. In 1833 the New England Convention was reconstituted as the General Convention of Universalists in the United States, an umbrella organization designed to include all the state conventions. By the early 1840s Universalists were claiming 853 societies and 512 clergy, with "600,000 of the population under their influence." Though this last figure was undoubtedly created out of thin air in a moment of euphoria, there certainly had been a remarkable growth during the preceding quarter century. The period was marked not only by vigorous growth but also by theological controversy. Controversy with the orthodox was to be expected, but the major controversy that broke out within the Universalist ranks was not. It started innocently enough when, in 1817, Ballou and Edward Turner, two of the four members of the Gloucester Conference study group, decided it would be a worthwhile theological exercise to debate the subject of future punishment, that is, whether those who died would be punished for their sins before entering heaven. Ballou, who was undecided on the question and considered it of marginal importance, agreed to argue against the existence of future punishment, with Turner arguing in favor. It was agreed that the debate would be reported in detail in the *Gospel Visitant,* a Universalist journal devoted to theological discussion.

In the debate Turner stated that the basic question was whether "death necessarily produces such a moral change in the mind of the sinner, as to make him at once a willing, obedient and happy subject of the moral kingdom." If it could be proved from reason and Scripture that this was the case, then he would concede defeat. In taking up the challenge Ballou was forced to rethink his theology carefully. In the *Treatise* he had admitted that, since many people apparently do not die in a state of grace, it would be hard to defend the doctrine of universal salvation unless there was some change for the better after death. Many Universalists, John Murray and Elhanan Winchester among them, had argued in favor of future punishment on this basis, contending that the souls of the dead must undergo purification in hell before entering heaven. In his response to Turner, Ballou fell back on his theory of the two contrasting natures inherent in humanity. He argued that the carnal nature, inclined to sinfulness, is destroyed by death, while the spiritual nature, committed to moral goodness, survives.

The debate reached its climax when Turner asked Ballou how, given his position, he could interpret the passage in I Peter 3:18-20 that describes Christ as having "preached unto the spirits in prison." The usual Universalist interpretation was that Christ was preaching to those in hell who had died unreconciled and were thereby saved. In fact, Ballou himself had earlier offered such an interpretation, as Turner probably remembered. After pondering the passage, Ballou finally concluded that "the spirits in prison" simply referred to the Gentiles, to whom the resurrected Christ brought his message of salvation, an interpretation that in no sense implied the existence of future punishment. By this point in the debate he was convinced that he had met Turner's challenge— he felt he had demonstrated on the basis of reason and Scripture that the human soul is immediately purged of sin at death, and hence no future punishment is necessary, a conviction he would hold for the rest of his life.

Until this debate, Universalists had known there were differences among them over the matter of future punishment, but they had seen this as being of minor importance—their agreement that all would be saved, whether sooner or later, was enough to hold them together. During the debate, however, a note of hostility was interjected by a recently ordained minister named Jacob Wood. Wood, who had evidently taken a personal dislike to Ballou, published a pamphlet in which he vigorously attacked the latter's position. "I will not call those who [accept Ballou's position] *'stupid animals'*," he wrote, "but I really think the opinion very erroneous. The many gross absurdities . . . which it is calculated to produce, render it a doctrine justly deserving of disapprobation and contempt." He followed by quoting from letters by eleven other ministers (in most cases without their permission) to support his contention that "with but a *very few* exceptions" a belief in future punishment was held by the Universalist clergy. Two weeks after publication of the pamphlet, when the General Convention met at his church in Charlton, Massachusetts, Wood threatened to introduce a resolution at the meeting condemning the nonbelief in future punishment and to lead a secessionist movement if it failed to carry. As it developed, Wood never offered the resolution, but his strong opposition to Ballou and Ballou's position continued undiminished.

The debate between Ballou and Turner had been carried out in the pages of the *Gospel Visitant*, but when that journal ceased publication at the end of 1818, there was a lull in the controversy that lasted for several years. Soon after coming to Boston, Ballou and a parishioner, Henry Bowen, had started a newspaper, the *Universalist Magazine*, with Ballou as editor and Bowen as publisher. Ballou had been careful not to renew the debate through this new medium, feeling that it would be harmful to the Universalist cause. When he temporarily gave up the editorship in

1821 due to illness, however, his successor quickly took steps to revive the debate. Wood and others, writing under pseudonyms, entered the fray, and Ballou himself was soon drawn in. Eventually, Wood, writing under the name "Restorationist," proposed that each side choose a representative to write a statement supporting that side's position, that the two statements be published in the *Universalist Magazine* with no rebuttals permitted, and that the public be left to draw its own conclusions. Wood's role as peacemaker was badly compromised, however, by his appending the following to his proposal:

> If the advocates of the doctrine of *no* future misery are honourable and conscientious in their cause, they will be willing to meet us on this just and equal ground. It is wished that the gentleman who shall accept this invitation, will be one who is qualified to do full justice to his side of the question; and we hope that honor will restrain all others from interfering.

Ballou felt that the honor of the "Ultra-Universalists," as he and his followers had come to be known, had been unfairly attacked. Uncharacteristically, he lost his temper and responded heatedly that, if "Restorationist" would reveal his identity, he would explain why he would not accept the proposal and say what he thought of those who questioned his honor. A heated exchange followed, and Bowen, in an attempt to control the situation, finally asked Ballou to reassume the editorship. The latter agreed with the understanding that two of his young proteges, Hosea Ballou 2nd and Thomas Whittemore, would assist him as associate editors. The new editorial board announced that the *Universalist Magazine* would no longer be a vehicle for the debate, which had for the most part degenerated into personal attacks, but that communications on the important theological subject of future punishment would be welcomed. The hope that this new policy would put an end to hostilities turned out to be short-lived.

First, a piece submitted by Wood, writing again as "Restorationist," was edited in a way that he felt unfair. Then the editors refused to continue printing an ongoing exchange between Wood and one of the Ultra-Universalists after they got wind of a secret meeting at which Wood and his Restorationist allies had laid plans to publish an attack on the *Universalist Magazine* in another journal. The attack, written by Wood using his own name, appeared in the December 1822 issue of the *Christian Repository*. The article not only accused the *Universalist Magazine* editors of unfairness, but also charged the no-future-punishment "party" with forcing a view on the denomination that amounted to a *"modern corruption"* of Universalism—one that "lessens the motives to virtue, and gives force to the temptations of sin." Wood also claimed that the Restorationists had tried again and again for reconciliation with the Ultra-Universalists, only to have their overtures rejected, and he warned that "if a separation be the final result, *we* did not seek it, and *they* must be considered as its legitimate authors."

The two Ballous and Whittemore were quick to reply. After revealing the identity of the six ministers responsible for the attack, Edward Turner and Paul Dean among them, they reviewed the controversy, refuted Wood's claim that the Restorationists had worked for reconciliation, and condemned their devious tactics. Among other things, they accused Wood of having spread rumors that "nine-tenths of Br. Ballou's society are infidels" and Dean of having "reported, *secretly*, that Mr. Ballou retained nothing of Christianity but the name."

The Restorationists did not respond publicly. Instead, they met with Hosea 2nd and Whittemore (the elder Ballou was out of town), and an agreement was reached, to be published in the *Universalist Magazine*, that neither side had meant to impugn the honor and integrity of the other. This effort at reconciliation failed, however, when the elder Ballou, upset at what had taken place in his absence, refused, as senior editor, to print the statement. Quite predictably, the Restorationists got angry, and the old enmity was revived. The long friendship between Ballou and Turner, already severely strained, now ended, and Turner left the denomination to become a Unitarian minister. Dean also resigned his Universalist fellowship, though he soon reconsidered and, with Ballou's help, was reinstated; in time, however, he, too, left the denomination and eventually the ministry.

Although the issue of future punishment continued to be discussed in some quarters for several years thereafter, there was little controversy attached to it. In 1831, however, a small group of Restorationists, feeling they were being discriminated against by the New England Convention, broke away to form "a religious Community for the Defense and Promulgation of the doctrines of

Revelation in their original purity—to be known by the name of the 'Massachusetts Association of Universal Restorationists.' " Of the eight ministers involved, only Paul Dean and Charles Hudson had taken part in the earlier debate. The group maintained that the majority of the New England Convention had departed from the faith of Murray, Winchester, and "the ancient Authors who have written on the subject" and argued "that Regeneration—a general Judgement, Future Rewards and Punishments, to be followed by the final Restoration of all mankind to holiness and happiness, are fundamental articles of Christian faith, and that the modern sentiments of No-Future accountability, connected with Materialism, are unfriendly to pure religion and subversive to the best interests of society."

The delegates to the New England Convention, meeting soon after the new association was organized, denied that the Restorationists had been unfairly treated and pointed out that the Winchester Profession, accepted as providing the theological norm for the convention, was written in broad enough terms to include both Ultra-Universalists and Restorationists. The members of the new association remained apart, however, and at their second annual meeting, held in Boston in January 1833, adopted a profession of faith of their own, identical to the Winchester Profession except for the addition, in the third article, of a clause affirming belief "in a retribution beyond death." Adin Ballou, a distant cousin of the two Hoseas, was the association's chief spokesperson; as editor of the *Independent Messenger*, later given the subtitle *Restorationist Advocate*, he carried on a battle of words with Thomas Whittemore, who by then was editing his own newspaper.

The Association of Universal Restorationists met annually for ten years, adding twelve ministers during that time, but by the last meeting in 1841, most of them had drifted away, some to the Unitarians. Adin Ballou, who convened the meeting, described the association as having fallen "quietly asleep, to wake no more." Thus, after a quarter of a century, ended the great Restorationist controversy, as it came to be known. In retrospect, it is evident that the controversy was fueled more by issues of personality and power than by theological differences. Many Universalists, both lay and clergy, were not very interested in these differences, and most of the Restorationists stayed in the denomination. After Hosea Ballou's death in 1852, the Restorationist view gradually became the majority position; it had been largely through the power of Ballou's preaching and personality that Ultra-Universalism had attained its predominance in the first place.

A major force in spreading the Universalist message during this period was provided by the many periodicals that sprang up throughout the country. Before Ballou came to Boston, there had been at least seven attempts to establish such publications, the first in 1793; but not until 1819, when Ballou himself founded the *Universalist Magazine*, did the denominational press begin to make an important impact. The magazine, through several mergers and under a variety of names and editors, has remained in existence ever since, currently as the *World*, the official journal of the Unitarian Universalist Association; it is one of the oldest continuously published periodicals in American religious history. In 1828 it merged with a newly established newspaper, the *Trumpet*, to form the *Trumpet and Universalist Magazine*, with Thomas Whittemore as editor, a position he was to hold until his death in 1861.

Whittemore had little formal education and was working as a bootmaker's apprentice when he was converted to Universalism by Hosea Ballou, soon after the latter came to Boston. Ballou took the young man under his wing, trained him for the ministry, and appointed him one of the associate editors of the magazine. Whittemore, with his keen mind and boundless energy, soon launched into careers in both ministry and journalism, and, as editor of the *Trumpet and Universalist Magazine*, quickly became one of the most influential figures in the denomination. A short, pugnacious man and a skilled controversialist, he tirelessly promoted Universalism (particularly the Ultra-Universalist cause) and defended it against all comers, especially Unitarians, of whom he had an abiding suspicion.

Whittemore was not only energetic, he was versatile. He served in the Massachusetts legislature, where he led a successful fight to disestablish the Congregational Church; he became president of both the Vermont & Massachusetts Railroad and the Cambridge Bank; he was a musician and composer of hymns; he was a powerful preacher and temperance lecturer with "a frame of iron, and lungs of brass"; he was the main force behind the founding of the Universalist Historical Society; he wrote and published several books, among them *The Modern History of Universalism* and a biography of his mentor, Hosea Ballou. It was to the *Trumpet*, however, that he gave his greatest energy, making it Universalism's leading (and loudest) voice.

The *Trumpet and Universalist Magazine* was only one of a large number of Universalist periodicals that existed (many of them only briefly) during this period. Sylvanus Cobb's *Christian Freeman*, published in Massachusetts from 1839 until it merged with the *Trumpet* in 1862, stands out as perhaps the most important of the rest; it advertised itself as "decidedly committed to the moral reforms of the day, such as Anti-Slavery and Temperance." Then, too, there was the *Southern Pioneer* from Baltimore; the *Liberalist* from Wilmington, North Carolina; the *Messenger of Glad Tidings* from Wetumpka, Alabama; the *Evangelical Magazine and Gospel Advocate* from Utica, New York; the *Western Evangelist* from Buffalo; and many more. Their large number sometimes made it difficult for a newcomer to the field to find a suitable title, and hence such names as *Primitive Expounder, Genius of Truth,* and *Banner of Love* appeared. In the mid-1840s there were some twenty-five to thirty Universalist newspapers being published, but a much larger number had been started, only to go out of business. According to Russell Miller, a total of 138 periodicals were launched between 1820 and 1850. They served, in Miller's words,

> . . .as a channel of communication, and often comfort, for hundreds of readers who were Universalists in sentiment or sympathy as well as profession, who were scattered in the vastness of a still predominantly rural and isolated America. In dozens of hamlets, villages, and cross-roads settlements which did not possess organized religious societies or could not afford the luxury of a settled preacher, the newspaper was the only link to a larger religious world.

The utility of these newspapers was not confined, of course, to rural America. In urban centers, as well, they provided their readers with denominational news, notices of upcoming meetings, inspirational readings, and stimulating theological discussion. During the second quarter of the nineteenth century, especially, they played an important and necessary role in Universalist denominational life.

As their denomination grew in strength, Universalists began to recognize that their commitment to "practice good works" applied not only to their daily living as individuals but also to their impact on society. One of the first arenas in which they determined to make such an impact was that of education. American education was going through a significant transition during the second quarter of the nineteenth century; the private schools that had sprung up to meet local needs were being replaced by a system of tax-supported public schools. The great majority of Universalists strongly supported this change, in large part because they felt that most of the private schools were promoting orthodox religious beliefs; hence, they welcomed the idea of public schools, which operated under the principle of church-state separation, where no religious instruction would be permitted. The Universalists were determined that nonsectarian education would be available during this period of transition. In addition to working for the establishment of public schools, they closely monitored the existing private schools, publicly criticizing those engaged in sectarian religious education, and they worked to establish their own nonsectarian schools, mostly residential secondary schools or "academies." Their record in trying to accomplish this latter goal was a mixed one—many of their plans never materialized, and many of the schools they did establish failed because of a lack of financial support; but others succeeded and made a significant contribution to American education.

Nichols Academy, established in Dudley, Massachusetts, in 1819, and Westbrook Seminary, established in Portland, Maine, in 1839, still exist, though both have passed out of Universalist hands. The Clinton Liberal Institute in Clinton, New York, operated from 1831 until 1900, when a major fire forced its closing. Most of the other academies (there were roughly a score of them) were relatively short-lived because of inadequate funds. Except for Nichols, all these Universalist schools were coeducational from the beginning, and all were determinedly non-sectarian. As Edward Turner told the students at Nichols, Universalist-sponsored schools were established as "nurseries of sound sense, sound morality, and sound learning," not as a means of sectarian indoctrination; the constitution of the Clinton Liberal Institute went so far as to enjoin that "no minister, of any denomination, shall have liberty to perform the services of public worship within the Institute, on any occasion whatever." Students who wished to attend services in the village had their choice of four denominations—Baptist, Methodist, Presbyterian, and Universalist. In keeping with their nonsectarian nature, these schools, with one brief exception, never used the word "Universalist" in their names, preferring to use the term "liberal" instead. However, there was no objection to religious education per se. Although Sunday schools didn't gain popularity until the second half of the century, a number of churches, with the encouragement of their state conventions and associations, organized such schools earlier, and many others provided catechisms for the instruction of children by their parents at home. In addition, an attempt was made in the early 1840s to establish a Universalist theological school in Medford, Massachusetts, to be called the "Walnut Hill Evangelical Seminary." The plan failed because of lack of financial support and Hosea Ballou's opposition—he felt that a call to preach and a determination to succeed were all that a Universalist minister needed. The formal training of ministers had to wait for another decade.

Other reforms also engaged Universalists during this period. In keeping with resolutions passed at the Philadelphia Convention in 1790, some Universalists spoke out for the abolition of slavery and war; others worked for temperance, women's rights, prison reform, the rehabilitation of prisoners, and the abolition of capital punishment. The greatest denominational involvement in these issues lay ahead, however. A radical reform movement that attracted some limited Universalist support in this period was associationism, an attempt in the first half of the nineteenth century to effect a basic change in society by establishing utopian socialistic communities. While these communities attracted only a small minority of Universalists—most of those in the movement were secularists Shakers, and members of other unorthodox Christian sects—they are significant because they marked the first attempt by Universalists to establish the kingdom of God on earth, a goal that would become increasingly important in Universalist thought. Horace Greeley, the editor of the New York *Tribune* and an active Universalist layperson, was a strong supporter of Brook Farm, the community founded in West Roxbury, Massachusetts, by Unitarian Transcendentalists, and a number of Universalists were involved in communities near Rochester and Watertown in upstate New York. However, by far the most important such enterprise with Universalist connections was the Hopedale Community in Massachusetts.

Adin Ballou had left the parish ministry to organize the community in 1842, soon after the demise of the Association of Universal Restorationists. It was to be "a compact neighborhood or village of practical christians, dwelling together by families in love and peace, insuring for themselves the comforts of life by agriculture and mechanical industry, and devoting the entire residue of their intellectual, moral and physical resources to the christianization and general welfare of the human race." Thirty-two people, including thirteen couples, most of them Restorationists, signed the initial membership list. Communal worship was a regular part of communal life, and all members subscribed to a *Standard of Practical Christianity*, which "was intended to cover the whole ground of personal and social righteousness." In doing so, they renounced not only intemperance, war, and slavery, but also licentiousness, covetousness, worldly ambition, exploitation, gossip, rash judgments, idleness, rudeness, overindulgence of every kind, unholy lusts, oathswearing, blasphemy, hasty marriages, proselytism, corporal punishment, cruelty to animals, and even participation in civil government! Unlike other utopian communities, "Fraternal Community No. 1," as it was called in anticipation of an ever-growing number of such ventures, was organized as a joint stock company with Ballou as President. The community bought a 258-acre farm, erected buildings, established a school, and began truck gardening. Gradually, operations expanded to include farming, orcharding, printing, cabinetmaking, and the manufacture of soap, hats, shoes, farm implements, loom temples, and boot-lasting apparatus. Members worked for the community for set wages and boarded in community-owned facilities. Food, shelter, light, heat, washing and ironing, and some medical care were provided at established rates. The members divided the profits on the basis of the amount of money invested and the work performed.

Controversies soon broke out among the members over individual rights, necessitating several changes. The requirement that all members live in community-owned housing was eliminated, as was the standard wage for all workers, and profits of the stock company began to be distributed solely on the basis of the amount of stock owned. A few members resigned in protest, feeling that the basic idea of community had been compromised in favor of individualism. Then a sexual liaison scandalized the community; the culprits were banished but found haven in a free-love association on Long Island called "Modern Times." By and large, however, the community prospered and grew, with the membership rising to more than 100. By 1852 Ballou felt confident enough about the future to relinquish the presidency and devote his time to missionary activity. Within a few years, however, the new president and his brother, who together had acquired a majority of the stock, found the community facing a financial crisis. As a result, they took over the community's property, paid off its liabilities, and established their own manufacturing company, based in what had become, almost overnight, a model industrial village.

As Ballou later wrote, "The Hopedale Community, as . . . an attempt to realize the Kingdom of God on earth, for which so many of us had prayed and toiled and sacrificed for so many years, had become a thing of the past—had been transformed into a mere religious, moral reform, and mutual guarantee association." Though deeply disappointed, Ballou was not bitter. He concluded that the experiment was too far ahead of the times to have succeeded, and he remained at Hopedale for the rest of his life, in time becoming minister of the local Unitarian church. In a sermon read at his own funeral in 1890 and written by himself for that occasion, Ballou stated that he had "left the world under a very strong assurance from Heaven that a regenerate and Christlike form of the Church will ere long be developed to prosecute this work of grand Social Reform."

In addition to Ballou, one other well-known Universalist minister, Abner Kneeland, became involved in the associationist movement, but only after he had renounced Universalism, become a freethinker, and spent sixty days in jail for blasphemy. William Ellery Channing, the Unitarian leader, had tried unsuccessfully to intervene in his behalf on the grounds of freedom of speech and of the press. After Kneeland's release in 1838, he moved to Iowa to organize a free-thought community, but it soon failed. He died there in 1844 at the age of seventy.

Although a majority of Universalists were Unitarian in their theology, and some Restorationist ministers had found their way into the Unitarian fold, the gap between the two denominations remained wide during the years of Hosea Ballou's Boston ministry. For one thing, the idea of universal salvation held little appeal for most Unitarians; more important, the social and educational chasm between the two groups was far too broad to be easily bridged. Ballou's *A Treatise on Atonement*, though well reasoned, was written in a style quite foreign to readers with Harvard educations, and his preaching style likewise seemed rough and unrefined. A student from the Boston Latin School, on hearing Ballou preach in 1825, gave this example of his pronunciation: "Brethering, I perceed to dev-il-ope and illusterate the follerin' p'ints." The breadth of the chasm between the two groups is illustrated by the fact that Ballou and William Ellery Channing, the leaders of the two denominations, were not personally acquainted with each other even though they lived and ministered in the same city for a quarter of a century! There were other differences between the two—Channing favored the continued establishment of the Congregational churches while Ballou did not; and Channing strongly opposed Ultra-Universalism, considering it an "irrational doctrine." Moreover, he pronounced "the growth of Universalism as the most threatening moral evil in our part of the country." Nevertheless, Ballou always held Channing in the highest regard despite their differences.

The Boston years were busy ones for Ballou. He refined his theology, revising his *Treatise* in the process, and continued his heavy involvement in denominational affairs. When the body of John Murray was exhumed from the Sargent plot in the Granary Burying Ground in Boston and reburied at Mt. Auburn Cemetery in Cambridge, Ballou offered the prayer of interment. (Murray's old church, the First Universal Society, had by this time been renewed, incidentally, under the able ministry of Sebastian Streeter.) Above all, Ballou's work at the School Street Church kept him well occupied. In time, though, dissatisfaction began to develop in the congregation. Ballou was growing old (he had reached seventy in 1841), and a growing number of members felt they needed younger leadership. Accordingly, a search was begun for an associate minister, but in time, some members became impatient and withdrew their support. With a financial crisis developing, Ballou realized that the church could not afford to support two ministers and graciously offered to step down, asking that he be given the title of senior minister without pay. In September 1845, the congregation voted to accept his offer and extended a call to Edwin Chapin, the young minister of the Charlestown church. Chapin accepted, and four months later he was installed; Ballou preached the sermon. Even though his days as the leader of the Universalist denomination had, in a real sense, come to an end, Hosea Ballou could look back with satisfaction on what had been accomplished. He would live for another six years, deeply honored and respected as "Father Ballou," the "elder statesman" of Universalism. When he died, there were many tributes, none more apt than that of the great Unitarian preacher, Theodore Parker, who said:

He went through the land proclaiming this great truth, and he has wrought a revolution in the thoughts and minds of men more mighty than any which has been accomplished during the same time by all the politicians of the nation.

Chapter Four

"To Begin a Better State of Things"

Confronting the Problems
of the Times, 1846–1869

In 1847, Hosea Ballou 2nd preached the occasional sermon to the General Convention of Universalists meeting in New York City. It was time, he said, for Universalists to start addressing both their own needs and the needs of the society—namely, higher education, including the sounder preparation of ministers, and the pressing social issues of the day. If they did not, he warned, they would not only see a steady flow of defectors from their ranks, but they would also be condemned for not practicing what they preached. "We must stand forth before the world," he insisted, "either as the active patrons, or the practical discouragers, of general improvement." His greatuncle undoubtedly disapproved of these sentiments; the elder Ballou opposed not only theological seminaries, but direct church involvement in social reform. The Universalist Church's task, he firmly believed, was to bring people to a correct understanding of God. Once that was accomplished, the rest would necessarily follow.

Looking back from the perspective of the 1880s, Richard Eddy agreed with the younger Ballou that the denomination had needed to take stock of itself at this time. He concluded his history, *Universalism in America*, with these words:

It would seem from the foregoing pages of this volume, that from 1820 to 1840 was the period in which Universalists were most active and aggressive. And to the careless reader or superficial observer, it may also seem that since that time no great progress has been made; that possibly there has been a retrograde movement, especially in point of numbers. It is true that the period indicated above was one of great activity and of apparent prosperity, but not of substantial growth in things essential to denominational permanence.... Our abiding growth dates from the time of our development of organized power.... Within less than two score years we have made our real, our lasting gains.

Despite the lack of reliable statistics, it is generally agreed that the rapid growth of Universalism slowed appreciably during the 1840s, and that after 1850, while there may have been some increase in an absolute sense, it was proportionately less than that of the country's population as a whole. Opposition to the doctrine of universal salvation was gradually subsiding, and this meant that the Universalist message was losing some of its radical appeal.

In this new climate the denomination was ready to heed the younger Ballou's advice and address its own needs. Almost at once attempts were made to strengthen the General Convention, which until then had played only an advisory role in its relations with the state conventions. By 1853 so many suggestions had been made for amending the convention's constitution that a special committee was appointed to come up with a plan "for the more perfect organization of the denomination." Two years later, a new constitution was adopted that attempted to establish the jurisdiction of the General Convention over the state conventions; the latter, however, by and large ignored the changes and continued to hold on to their power.

One change resulting from this denominational stocktaking, which made a far greater impact, was the adoption by the General Convention in 1848 of a Statement of Faith to which all candidates for the ministry were required to subscribe. The statement, presaging a general shift to conservatism in the denomination, required "the recognition and acknowledgment of the Bible as containing a special revelation from God, sufficient for faith and practice." The Universalist leadership had been keeping close tabs on what was happening in Unitarian circles, and undoubtedly the uproar caused by Ralph Waldo Emerson's Divinity School Address and Theodore Parker's sermon on "The Transient and Permanent in Christianity" prompted them to try to close the door on Transcendentalism and German Rationalism. The majority of ministers, including the two

Ballous and Whittemore, were solidly in favor of the statement; only a few left the denomination in protest.

The appeal by Hosea Ballou 2nd for the establishment of institutions of higher learning, whose programs would include the training of ministers, prompted an immediate positive response. Despite the elder Ballou's objections to formal theological education, a majority of the Universalist leadership saw that an increasingly well-educated laity required an increasingly well-educated clergy. A fund-raising drive to establish a college was quickly inaugurated, with the goal of $100,000 reached by 1851. Phineas T. Barnum, the showman and entrepreneur, was among the contributors; he was to be a generous supporter of the college for the rest of his life.

A number of building sites were considered for the institution— Medford, Franklin, Worcester, and Springfield in Massachusetts and Brattleboro in Vermont. Medford was finally chosen, over the objections of the younger Ballou, who felt it was too close to Harvard University and not only would suffer from comparison, but also would be subject to the questionable influence of Unitarians. One of the deciding factors was the offer of twenty acres of land by Charles Tufts, for whom Tufts College was eventually named. A charter was granted in 1852, and classes began two years later with a student body of seven and a faculty of three. Hosea Ballou 2nd agreed to serve as President after the trustees failed to meet the salary demands of their first choice. He was officially installed in August 1855, a "great day for Universalists . . . the great event in our denominational history." From then until his death in 1861, Ballou, in addition to his administrative responsibilities, regularly taught two courses, conducted Sunday services, and acted as college librarian.

In those early years the college was constantly in financial trouble, but it nevertheless managed to survive. By 1859 the student body had grown to seventy, and the number increased slowly but steadily thereafter. In a departure from usual Universalist practice, the college initially was not coeducational; it was not until the 1890s that women were admitted. Nor was there a theological school at Tufts in the beginning as had originally been planned; until 1869 students preparing for the ministry had to supplement their regular academic training with informal instruction in sermon preparation and delivery. The founding of Tufts College indeed marked "a great day for Universalists," a kind of coming of age for the denomination; its survival and growth gave evidence that Universalists not only had great plans but also had the strength and perseverance to make those plans a reality. In contrast to Tufts, St. Lawrence University, which received its charter in 1856, had a theological school from the beginning. In fact, the original plan of the New York State Convention had been to establish only a theological school, but when the town of Canton, located in the extreme northern part of the state, offered $15,000— more than any other municipality—to be chosen as the site, it did so with the stipulation that a nonsectarian college of letters and science be established there as well. The theological school began inauspiciously; only four students enrolled, and the inaugural ceremonies in 1858 were held at the local Universalist church during a late spring snowstorm. Ebenezer Fisher, a self-educated clergyman who was for several years the school's principal and only faculty member, had a very flexible admissions policy; all that was required was "a good English education" (interpreted quite broadly) and a desire to enter the Universalist ministry. By 1860 the student body had grown to twenty-two, and although the school always had financial troubles and was handicapped by its isolated location, it managed to survive until 1965, when the Unitarian-Universalist merger dictated its closing. The theological school and the college operated under a single board of trustees until 1910, and both were coeducational from the start. Olympia Brown, usually recognized as the first woman in America to receive full denominational ordination, entered the theological school in 1861 despite Fisher's efforts to dissuade her, and graduated two years later, with Fisher participating in her ordination.

In addition to Tufts and St. Lawrence, three other colleges, all coeducational, were founded by Universalists in the third quarter of the nineteenth century: Lombard University in Galesburg, Illinois; Buchtel College in Akron, Ohio; and Smithson College in Logansport, Indiana. Lombard, originally incorporated in 1851 as the Illinois Liberal Institute, was rechartered as a college in 1857, when it was also renamed for a major benefactor. Later, in 1881, the Ryder Divinity School was established as part of the college. After moving to Chicago in 1912, it was eventually absorbed by Meadville Theological School, a Unitarian seminary that had also relocated there. Degrees from the school, now known as Meadville/ Lombard, are granted under the Lombard charter. Lombard's other programs continued to operate at Galesburg until 1930, when the Great Depression forced the school to merge with Knox

College, its Galesburg neighbor.

Buchtel College, chartered in 1870 and named for its chief financial supporter, was controlled by the Ohio State Convention throughout most of its existence. It never fully recovered from a fire that destroyed the main building in 1899, after which the school became increasingly a community rather than a Universalist enterprise. In 1913, after a failed attempt to save Buchtel's Universalist identity through a merger with Lombard, the college became part of the University of Akron.

Smithson College, chartered in 1871 and, like Tufts, Lombard, and Buchtel, named for a major benefactor, opened its doors in 1872 with high hopes, great enthusiasm, and little else. In doing so Indiana Universalists were disregarding the warning of the 1870 General Convention against the founding of a new college without firm financial backing. Never attracting more than ninety students and never adequately funded, Smithson was forced to close for financial reasons just seven years after it began holding classes. Its main building, by then occupied by a teacher training school, was destroyed by fire in the 1890s, a common fate for buildings in those days.

Later, in 1891, Universalists would found the Throop Polytechnic Institute in Pasadena, California, but the school passed out of denominational control three years later; in time it became one of the country's major engineering schools, the California Institute of Technology. Overall, Universalist educational enterprises had mixed success, but as Russell Miller has pointed out, by 1870 "Universalists were operating no less than fifteen educational institutions—five colleges or universities, three professional schools (two for theology and one for law), and seven academies. . . . It was indeed an impressive record, all things considered."

While the first thrust of Hosea Ballou 2nd's sermon to the General Convention in 1847 had been a call to his fellow Universalists to meet the denomination's need for colleges and seminaries, the second thrust had been a call to address the pressing social issues of the day. The New England Universalist General Reform Association had been organized the year before to evaluate the many reform movements that had sprung up and to support those it judged most worthy; Ballou's sermon urged his fellow delegates to support such efforts throughout the denomination. The effect of Ballou's words is impossible to judge, but, for whatever reason, the Reform Association grew in strength, dropped the words "New

England" from its title, and expanded its membership to include all Universalists who wished to pay the fifty-cent dues. The scope of the association's concerns was indeed broad, with no less than forty areas of concern identified in four major categories:

1. *Economic and Domestic Relations.* Slavery and the Colored Race; Domestic Slave Trade; Service; Wages; Marriage; Women's Rights; Parental Relations; Rights to the Soil.

2. *International Relations.* War; Non-Resistance; Diplomacy; Commerce; Seamen; Foreign Slave Trade; Colonization; Indians; Foreign Relations; Conflict of Races.

3. *Social Institutions and Habits.* Temperance; Education; the Pulpit; the Sabbath; the Press; Politics and Laws; Amusements; the Poor; Dress; Food.

4. *Offenders, Irresponsible and Unfortunate Persons.* Capital Punishment; Prison Discipline; Juvenile Offenders; Imprisonment for Debt; Dueling; Gambling; Courts; Trials; Idiots; Insane; Deaf and Dumb.

To prioritize the list must have been a staggering task, if indeed it was even attempted! The elder Ballou would not have approved of what the Reform Association was doing, but by the time the list was drawn up in 1857, he had been dead for some five years.

It is evident that slavery was one of the social issues, if not *the* social issue, that concerned members of the Reform Association the most. To be sure, only a small fraction of Universalists belonged to the association, but their concern for the abolition of slavery was reflected throughout the denomination, even if with less of an activist emphasis. Earlier in the 1820s and 1830s, Universalists had generally condemned slavery as inconsistent with their theology and its idea of an all-inclusive human family, considering it a social evil that must slowly be eradicated as individual minds and hearts were changed. They recalled with pride the strong condemnations of slavery by de Benneville, Rush, and the 1790 Philadelphia Convention, and pointed out that one of the original members of Murray's church in Gloucester was a former slave. Nevertheless, most Universalists thought it both inappropriate and divisive to

An influential Universalist layperson, Mary A. Livermore (1820-1905) was a lecturer and leader in the women's rights movement.

make the abolition of slavery an item for denominational action.

By 1840, however, the climate had changed enough for a Universalist Anti-Slavery Convention to be held at Lynn, Massachusetts, with thirty-four people attending. Among the twelve resolutions adopted were ones condemning slaveholders as "in the sight of God guilty of theft and robbery" and affirming the right to "reform error in practice and law" by peaceful means. Three years later, at the General Convention in Akron, Ohio, the delegates put the denomination as a whole on record as condemning slavery as "contrary to the plainest dictates of natural justice and Christian love, . . . [and to] that doctrine of Universal Grace and Love which we cherish as the most important of revealed truth." The somewhat unexpected passage of this resolution delighted some and dismayed others, with the strongest protests predictably coming from Universalists in the Deep South. The South Carolina Convention, at its meeting in 1841, expressed its disapproval "of any interference with the subject of negro Slavery by the people of those States where it does not exist; and we *solemnly protest* against any action on that subject by the brethren of our order."

But despite the dissenters, the abolitionist movement within the denomination, though never radical, continued to grow stronger over the years. Mary Livermore, who was later to rise to prominence both as a lecturer and promoter of women's rights, observed slavery firsthand while serving as a teacher for three years on a Virginia plantation; she returned north "a pronounced abolitionist, accepting from no one any apology for slavery" and with deep sympathy for all who were caught up in its system, whether black or white. She and her husband, Daniel, a Universalist minister, became outspoken advocates of abolition, first in Daniel's parishes and later through their newspaper.

Universalist ministers had an advantage over their Unitarian counterparts in speaking out on the subject, especially in New England, where much of the textile industry was controlled by wealthy Unitarians. When the fugitive slave Thomas Sims was captured in Boston in 1851, William Lloyd Garrison's *Liberator* reported: "The bells of the Orthodox, Methodist, and Universalist churches in Waltham were tolled on Saturday when the news of the man stealing was received. The bell on the Unitarian Church being clogged with cotton would not sound." Even so, many Universalist ministers found themselves in trouble with their congregations for preaching too often and too strongly on the subject.

Passage of the Kansas-Nebraska Act in 1854, allowing the extension of slavery into the territories, strengthened abolitionist sentiment among Northern Universalists who adopted resolutions in protest. At the same time the differences between the Northern majority in the denomination and the badly outnumbered Southern minority were further increased. The Georgia State Convention even went so far as to "disclaim having any connection with the Universalists of the North, further than faith in an entire world's salvation" and to recommend "the speedy organization of a distinct Body, to be known as the Southern Convention." Such a convention was actually organized in 1858, but with a clause in its constitution that it be "subordinate to the General Convention," a proviso that the Georgia, Mississippi, and South Carolina State Conventions soon disclaimed. The intersectional battle of words carried over to the denominational press, with John C. Burruss of the *Universalist Herald* and Sylvester Cobb of the *Christian Freeman* hurling insults at each other. A partial truce was finally called when Burruss agreed to stop printing slave-trading advertisements in his paper. In the end, the Universalists, unlike a number of Protestant denominations, did not formally split over the slavery issue. Their commitment to inclusiveness had perhaps helped to hold them together. Russell Miller calls the impact of Universalist efforts in the struggle against slavery

> . . .difficult to determine. But the record is clear that their efforts were extensive, and their willingness to commit themselves officially as a denomination, even at the risk of disunion, is testimony to their courage and their concern for freedom. The battle had been waged on two fronts: to win over the majority of Universalists to the cause; and to help persuade whoever would listen and read that slavery was a great moral blot on the national escutcheon. Even more, it was contrary to the basic teachings of the denomination and raised problems more enduring and more sensitive than legal bondage. Universalists eager for the abolition of slavery repeatedly insisted that . . . there was an even larger challenge to be met. . . . To make really meaningful the abolition of slavery, . . . [people] 'must conquer [their] miserable prejudices.' Only then could true social justice be achieved.

With the outbreak of the Civil War in 1861, Northern Universalists quickly affirmed their support for the Union, blaming the South and slavery for the war and seeing force as necessary to put down the rebellion. In their Chicago newspaper, Daniel and Mary Livermore condemned Jefferson Davis, President of the Confederacy, as a traitor. Even John Burruss opposed secession as "suicidal"; probably as a result, his newspaper was soon out of business, at least for the duration of hostilities. The 1863 General Convention passed resolutions strongly supporting President Lincoln and his policies and calling for the arming of freed slaves to fight for the Union. Universalist men joined the Union armed forces in large numbers, and almost fifty ministers became chaplains. A number of Universalist women became nurses, among them Clara Barton, a member of a Universalist family from North Oxford, Massachusetts, who became known as "the angel of the battlefield" for her work with the soldiers; later, she founded the American Red Cross. Mary Livermore worked with Henry W. Bellows, the Unitarian minister who headed the United States Sanitary Commission, to organize a massive supply network for Union hospitals in the Midwest. While the Universalist churches in the North stayed busy supporting the war effort, many Universalist churches in the South were forced to close, some for good. The minister of the church in Richmond, Virginia, the only clergyman in the city to support the Union, was arrested, imprisoned, and finally given safe conduct across the Union lines; most Southern Universalists, however, supported the Confederacy.

After the war ended in 1865, Northern Universalists strongly supported the passage of the Civil Rights Act of 1866 and the 14th Amendment, and many volunteered to work with the Freedmen's Bureau. In Newberry, South Carolina, Henry Summer, a leading layperson, wrote a series of articles in the *Universalist Herald* (which had resumed publication under Burruss's editorship in 1867) calling for a new era of cooperation between North and South, blacks and whites. The long, slow process of reconciliation had at least begun.

During this period, the denomination's work in another important area, women's rights, focused on women's efforts to receive ordination to the ministry, a status they had not yet attained in any denomination before the Civil War. While a few women like Maria Cook had preached—and preached well—during the first half of the century, it was not until the national women's rights movement began to gain strength that Universalist pulpits really opened up to women. The Women's Rights Convention held in Worcester in 1850, just two years after the landmark meeting in Seneca Falls, New York, proved especially significant to Universalists because it brought the issue forcefully to their attention through the denominational press. Thomas Whittemore, editor of the influential *Trumpet*, was sarcastic in his report of the meeting:

> The Women had a Convention in Worcester, Mass. to assert their rights. . . . Some distinguished female talkers were there, whose husbands, at home, must have had a time of heavenly stillness during their absence. This is the only good, as far as we can see, that will grow out of the Convention. Judge not the women of Massachusetts by this motly assembly. . . .

Predictably, Whittemore would publicly object when he learned, just four months later, of a woman preaching from a Universalist pulpit. He wrote:

> We saw it stated in some of the Universalist papers . . . that 'Mrs. Lydia A. Jenkins, wife of a Universalist clergyman from Port Byron, N.Y., has commenced preaching to good acceptance.' . . . We have no occasion to have any disrespect personally to this woman preacher; but we regard her resolution to preach as unwise. It were better for her to remain at home and attend to her domestic duties.

Whittemore then went on to quote St. Paul: "Let your women keep silent in the churches; for it is not permitted them to speak. . . ." However, Jenkins kept right on preaching "to good acceptance," and in time Whittemore, hearing that she had been ordained, let the readers of the *Trumpet* know that this had certainly not been done with denominational sanction. Moreover, he felt compelled to say "that we doubt whether the denomination will approve the act of ordaining a woman as a preacher of the gospel and pastor of a Society." Whether Jenkins actually ever received ordination is not clear (there is no convincing evidence that she had), but she served with her husband in what can best be described as a successful parish co-ministry. When Whittemore finally heard her preach, even he became convinced of her ability, describing her sermon as "one of the most effective, tender, instructive, truthful discourses . . . that we have ever heard." Jenkins's reputation as a preacher quickly spread throughout the Northeast, and perhaps more than any other person, she prepared the way for women to be ordained to the Universalist ministry.

If the status of Jenkins's ordination remains uncertain, Olympia Brown's ordination in 1863 came with full denominational authority, and other women soon followed. By the time the 19th Amendment was passed in 1920, giving women the right to vote, a total of eighty-eight women had been ordained as Universalist ministers. With the exception of the Unitarians, who by then had ordained forty-two, other denominations were slow to follow suit. It would be another half century before the ordination of women became common in American church life. Now, in many denominations, the gates have been opened wide, but it was Jenkins, Brown, and their Universalist sisters who had shown the way more than a century earlier.

Closely allied to the issue of women's rights was the temperance movement, which originally advocated moderation in the use of alcoholic beverages, but soon moved on to condemn the use of all distilled spirits, as distinct from beer and wine, and finally promoted total abstinence from any form of alcohol. Originally, Universalists shared the same attitudes on the subject as most other Americans; John Murray, at Judith's urging, regularly drank wine for the sake of his health, and liquor was freely served at church meetings and to ministers making parish calls. It was not until the bad effects of overindulgence were becoming obvious around 1830 that Universalists joined people from other denominations in crusading for temperance. Women, though less prone to drinking alcoholic beverages than men, were nevertheless often victims of intemperance—not only victims of physical abuse by inebriated husbands but also victims of poverty resulting from squandered wages.

Mary Livermore and her husband, Daniel, Thomas Whittemore, Sylvanus Cobb, Adin Ballou, Horace Greeley, and historian Richard Eddy were among the many denominational leaders who worked for temperance, preaching, lecturing, writing, organizing temperance societies, and pressing for the passage of temperance resolutions and, eventually, for laws to restrict or prohibit the sale of intoxicants. In time the movement for total abstinence became so strong in the denomination that many churches replaced wine with water or grape juice in their communion services. Even Phineas T. Barnum, a *bon vivant* who prided himself on his fine wine collection, was persuaded to move from moderation to abstinence; after hearing a persuasive sermon on the subject, he went home and poured his whole collection down the drain! Denominational resolutions supporting Prohibition continued to be passed through the 1920s, when the failure of the 18th Amendment, ratified in 1919, became obvious.

The treatment of prisoners was another major concern of Universalist reformers, whose theology implied that all people, including criminals, were members of one human family and worthy of salvation, not only in the next world, but, insofar as possible, in this world as well. In the late eighteenth century, Benjamin Rush had argued forcefully on theological grounds for the better treatment of prisoners, including elimination of the death penalty:

A belief in God's universal love to all his creatures, and that he will finally restore all those of them that are miserable to happiness, is a *polar* truth. It leads to truths upon all subjects, more especially upon the subject of government. It establishes the *equality* of mankind—it abolishes the punishment of death for any crime—and converts jails into houses of repentance and reformation.

In the nineteenth century other Universalists took up the cause, prominent among them Charles Spear, who, after a brief career in the parish ministry, devoted his last thirty years to prison reform and the abolition of the death penalty. He visited prisoners, taught Sunday school classes to inmates (until the authorities discovered he was a Universalist), helped those who had been released from prison, gave countless lectures on the need for reform, and from 1845 until 1861 published the *Prisoners' Friend*, advertised as "the only journal known in the world that is wholly devoted to the Abolition of Capital Punishment and the Reformation of the Criminal." Spear, though gaining little public recognition for his efforts, nevertheless derived satisfaction from seeing prison conditions improve significantly during those thirty years and the death penalty abolished in three states and imposed less often in others. He and his wife Sarah, also a committed reformer, lived together on the edge of poverty, doing the work they felt called to do. Most Universalists, in keeping with their theology, strongly supported both prison reform and the abolition of the death penalty throughout the greater part of the nineteenth century and on into the twentieth. Today, these same concerns are kept alive in the Unitarian Universalist Association.

Not all the issues listed by the Universalist General Reform Association in 1857 had been addressed before 1870, but certainly many had been. Universalists had joined with members of a number of other denominations to work for temperance, the abolition of slavery, and the reform of prisons and mental institutions; they had played a small part in the pacifist and associationist movements; they had shared leadership with the Quakers and Unitarians in pressing for women's rights; and they had led the way in fostering coeducational institutions, the ordaining of women to the ministry, and the movement to abolish the death penalty. All in all, they had responded well to the challenge that Hosea Ballou 2nd had laid down for them at the General Convention in 1847.

Meanwhile, the basic work of the churches, associations, and conventions continued. There were children to be dedicated, couples to be married, the sick and distressed to be encouraged, the dead to be buried, sermons to be preached and heard, hymns to be sung, Sunday schools to be kept going, money to be raised, new members to be recruited, ministers to be educated and ordained. So, while the establishment of educational institutions and the reform of social institutions absorbed the attention of many Universalists during this period of denominational history, for most Universalists involvement in the life of their local churches, disrupted as it often was by the Civil War, continued to be central.

As the centennial of John Murray's coming to America approached, Universalists could look back and see how far they had come in a hundred years—from the new and hopeful gospel of an itinerant, unordained preacher to an established denomination with hundreds of churches and tens of thousands of members— although how many tens of thousands no one really knew. In the process, Universalists had evolved from a disorganized group of self-educated farmers and tradesmen into a powerful body of men and women that, while still including self-educated farmers and tradesmen, also included college presidents, bankers, newspaper editors, and wealthy entrepreneurs. Also in the process, the social, economic and educational gap between Universalists and Unitarians, so wide just a few decades earlier, had narrowed to the point that the two denominations could even explore a possible merger.

After the National Conference of Unitarian Churches was organized by Henry W. Bellows immediately after the end of the Civil War, Universalists were invited to discuss the possibility of their churches joining the new organization, presumably under an inclusive name. Following serious discussion, however, both parties agreed that the time was not yet ripe, that "in the present condition of things we must continue to act as two denominations, because the majority of both are not yet prepared for the union." Some years earlier, Thomas Starr King, who had fellowship as a minister in both denominations, had jokingly said that they were really "too near of kin to be married." When asked to explain the difference between them, he replied that the Universalists thought that God was too good to damn them forever, while the Unitarians thought that they were too good to be damned. The gap had narrowed enough for conversation to take place across it, but it was still far from closed.

Chapter Five

"No Doctrine Not Clearly Taught in the Bible"

The Denomination Grows Conservative, 1870–1892

When Universalists gathered at Gloucester in late September 1870 to mark the hundredth anniversary of John Murray's landing in America, it was the largest religious gathering that had ever taken place in the nation's history. For three days, a crowd estimated to have reached 12,000 listened to addresses, attended worship services, carried on the business of the General Convention, and broke bread and talked with one another. More than a hundred tents, the largest with a seating capacity of 5,000, served as meeting halls, as headquarters for the various organizations, and as housing and dining areas for those attending. However, these facilities proved inadequate to accommodate the unexpectedly large turnout; many had to find hospitality in local homes, and some of the larger meetings had to be held outdoors. Fortunately, the weather was fine, and a good spirit prevailed despite the inconveniences.

The record shows that 242 ministers were on hand (roughly one-third of those in fellowship), and among the throng of laypeople were such Universalist notables as Mary Livermore, Horace Greeley, Phineas T. Barnum, and former governor of Maine Israel Washburn. Livermore and Washburn both gave major addresses, as did the Rev. Alonzo A. Miner, who succeeded Hosea Ballou 2nd as president of Tufts after Ballou's death in 1861. Appropriately, special recognition was given to John Murray's place in the denomination's tradition. His pulpit robe was displayed by a delegate, who rhetorically called for someone who could fill it; a short memorial service was held at the building (by then a hay barn) that had housed the original Gloucester congregation; and the communion set that Murray had imported for his congregation was used in a special celebration of the Lord's Supper. The Reverend Edward Everett Hale brought greetings from the National Conference of Unitarian Churches, asserting that he had "no wish . . . to suggest, even by innuendo, any consolidation or fusion of the bodies here represented" and extolled what he saw to be "the finest illustration of the great Universal Church of the future, in the happy and friendly relations which . . . connected, in vital sympathy, the two liberal bodies of America." Liberal Christianity, he maintained, did not need any "mock fusion," but rather "a broad track" to carry its message on "two wheels." The audience evidently liked what they heard, for they interrupted Hale's brief address ten times with applause. The last important item of convention business was to appoint two representatives to carry fraternal greetings to "the next meeting of the American Unitarian Conference." One of the few disturbing notes in the centennial celebration was the lack of representation from the Southern churches; undoubtedly the breach caused by the war and the impoverishment of the South were obstacles still to be overcome.

The major accomplishment of the 116 official delegates to the business sessions of the Convention was their adoption of a new constitution to create a strengthened, more centralized organizational structure. Work toward this end had been going on for a dozen years, prompted by a growing dissatisfaction with the loose and ineffectual structure that had existed since 1833. The new constitution established a three-level hierarchy of General Convention, state convention, and parish (associations no longer were given official recognition). The delegates to each state convention would be the ministers within the convention (except for those "disabled by years or sickness"), lay delegates from the parishes, and the convention officers (previously, delegates had been chosen by the associations). The chief responsibility of a state convention was "Fellowship, Ordination and Discipline over the Universalist Clergymen and parishes within its territorial limits." In addition, each state convention was expected to "devote special attention to all matters of denominational concern," such as raising money, keeping statistics, supporting Sunday schools and missionary work, and caring for indigent ministers and their families.

The delegate body of the General Convention would comprise the presidents and secretaries of the various state conventions, together with, in most cases, one ministerial and two lay delegates from each convention, with provisions for additional representation from the larger ones. The Convention would elect a president and vice president annually, a board of trustees for four-year terms, and a secretary and a treasurer to serve its pleasure. While the General Convention was authorized to hold trust funds, raise money, and require reports from the state conventions and other organizations under its jurisdiction, it was chiefly to serve as an ultimate tribunal "by which shall be adjudicated all cases of dispute and difficulty between State Conventions, and a Court of Final Appeal before which may be brought cases of discipline and questions of government not provided for and settled by subordinate bodies."

The General Convention thus was defined as more of an ecclesiastical than an administrative body, operating in an organizational structure that was more presbyterian than congregational. Indeed, the Universalists, by making their associations and state conventions the ordaining and credentialing bodies, had departed from pure congregationalism early in their history.

The new constitution, and the "Laws for Securing a Uniform System of Fellowship, Government and Discipline" that accompanied it, affirmed the importance of the Winchester Profession by incorporating it as part of its contents, but it excluded the Liberty Clause that had been appended to it from the beginning. For the first time, assent to the Profession was made a specific requirement for ministerial fellowship. When this proposed departure from past practice came before the convention, only one delegate voiced an objection. What had for sixty-seven years been a very general statement adopted to meet the requirements of various state laws, had thus become something dangerously close to a creed. One can well imagine the objections that the delegates to the 1803 convention would have raised!

The Universalist denomination was following the pattern of many institutions—with time and growth it was not only becoming more highly organized, it was also becoming more conservative. The move toward organization and conservatism was in large part dictated by a growing understanding that the days of confrontation were ending. Other denominations were assimilating Universalist ideas and might soon take over the field unless the denomination consolidated its efforts and led the Church Universal toward its destiny. The times seemed to demand that independence of individual belief and local parish be sacrificed in the interest of maintaining one great united front.

It was not long before this new conservatism found expression in a dramatic way. Herman Bisbee had graduated from the theological school at St. Lawrence in 1864, a year after Olympia Brown, and, like her, had been ordained in Malone, New York. After graduation he moved with his family to St. Paul, Minnesota, where he soon became minister of the Universalist church in nearby St. Anthony.

At first his views were evidently well within the mainstream of Universalist thought, but after a sojourn in the Boston area he began to preach Emersonian "natural religion." Religion, he said, is "the effort which man makes to perfect himself, not the effort God makes to perfect him." His views soon were condemned in the denominational press as being in "the high and oracular fashion of our Boston Free Religionists," to which there could admittedly be no objection "provided he does not implicate the Universalist Church in it. Evidently he is no longer in sympathy with our denomination. We hope he does not, either in form or fact, pretend to be."

Bisbee replied that he had returned to St. Anthony at the urging of the congregation to resume his ministry there, that he was in ministerial fellowship and a strong supporter of the denomination. "I am a Universalist," he asserted. "I did not know that I was regarded as being other than a Universalist clergyman." He then asked for a retraction, stating that he had been unjustly attacked and that he was "so far sound in the faith, as to be worthy to retain my letter" of fellowship.

No retraction came; instead, an editorial described Bisbee as "a thoroughgoing infidel" who had ridiculed the Bible, and it called on the Minnesota State Convention to remove him from fellowship. "The Universalist Church is a Christian Church, unqualifiedly such," read the editorial. "No man has any business in its ministry who is not also a Christian, in faith as well as in character." Bisbee responded that he had entered the ministry with the clear understanding that it was quite sufficient to accept the Bible as containing a revelation, without accepting it as literally true or infallible, and he went on to attack the denomination's trend toward orthodoxy. Furthermore, he strenuously objected to being tried in the press rather than through official denominational channels.

Not long afterward, the Committee on Fellowship, Ordination, and Discipline of the Minnesota State Convention, acting on the complaint of "various persons, members of the Universalist Societies in Minneapolis, St. Paul and other parishes," began an investigation of Bisbee. Several months later, in June 1872, it presented a report charging Bisbee with "unministerial conduct" and recommending his removal from fellowship. The report stated that "in the name of Christianity and Universalism Mr. Bisbee has uttered doctrines subverting Christianity, and entirely contrary to the principles of the Universalist Church." After long discussion, the Minnesota State Convention, by a vote of 47 to 23, accepted the committee's recommendation.

Bisbee promptly submitted his resignation from the Universalist ministry and as minister of the St. Anthony church. His congregation, which had stood strongly behind him during the controversy, not only urged him to continue as its minister, but also changed its name to the First Independent Universalist Society, thus indicating its willingness to withdraw from the denomination, should that prove necessary. Bisbee stayed until the fall, when he again resigned, citing ill health.

It had been a difficult time for Bisbee (not only did he lose his fellowship, but his wife had died during the year), and he doubtless felt the need to move on. After a period of study at Harvard and Heidelberg universities, Bisbee returned to the ministry, this time as a Unitarian, to serve the Hawes Place Church in South Boston. Before this, however, he had appealed the decision of the Minnesota State Convention to the General Convention. A board of appeal appointed by the trustees upheld the Minnesota Convention's decision after carefully considering his case, and condemned Bisbee for a "general drift of doctrine . . . which is antagonistic to the conviction and express belief of the Universalist Church, and subversive of the integrity and influence of the denomination."

That same year, the editors of the *Universalist Register* published an essay, quite possibly inspired by the Bisbee affair, which caught the prevailing mood of the times. Titled "The Universalist Faith," it reviewed the origin and contents of the Winchester Profession and then strongly reaffirmed it as a necessary and Bible-based creed. "No doctrine which is not plainly taught in the Bible, or not fairly deducible therefrom forms any part of our faith as Universalists," the essay read. "Here we stand as a people, and here we have ever stood." The Profession had "proved to be a bond of unity and peace, and a source of power to us as a Christian denomination. . . . A church without a creed is smitten with paralysis, is in a false position before the world, and will be inefficient for great and critical emergencies."

The Universalists who had convened at Winchester, New Hampshire, in 1803 would have been amazed (and some of them outraged) to hear their broad statement of belief described as a creed, but, with the Liberty Clause now removed, that is what it was rapidly becoming in the minds of many. Except for the deletion of the Liberty Clause, the Profession had remained unchanged ever since its adoption; but now, seen in this new light, attempts were soon made to refine it further.

When, in 1875, Abel C. Thomas of Philadelphia objected to the phrase "finally restore" in Article the Second, he opened a veritable Pandora's box. Over the next decade a number of proposals (all defeated) were made to replace the verb "restore" with "bring," "lead," "come," "attain," or "save." Then objections arose to the word "holiness." At the 1884 General Convention a special committee proposed that both the phrases "finally restore" and "holiness and happiness" be omitted, so that the last clause of the article would read "save the whole family of mankind," but that proposal failed, too.

Meanwhile, many Universalists were becoming exasperated that so much time and energy was being expended in this way, convinced that the General Convention had more important things to do; the problem, however, would not go away. In 1887, another committee proposed a whole new Statement of Belief, born of compromise. A. A. Miner, the respected former president of Tufts, reminded the delegates that the controversy that had begun a dozen years earlier over a single word had now taken the form of "a profound revolution—a complete reconstruction," which he found to be "clumsy, wholly lacking in the wisdom which constructed the old Profession."

After two years of prolonged debate, the "complete reconstruction" was finally rejected, and by 1891 many Universalists had come to two conclusions: first, that the old Profession could never be reworded in a way that would gain broad approval; and second, that no new statement could be created on which all Universalists would agree. At least for this particular denomination of Christians, creedmaking had been found to be an almost impossible task!

The trend toward greater organization within the denomination, illustrated most obviously by the restructuring dictated by the new constitution, also appeared in other ways. In 1889, for example, the numerous youth groups affiliated with local churches were organized into the national Young People's Christian Union (YPCU), which, under a variety of names and structures, has survived continuously until the present day. The current organization, known as Young Religious Unitarian Universalists (YRUU), is the successor to Liberal Religious Youth (LRY), which resulted from the merger of the American Unitarian Youth and the Universalist Youth Fellowship in 1953, eight years before the merger of their parent denominations. A total of 131 delegates from fifty-six societies and thirteen states attended the organizational meeting of the YPCU held in Lynn, Massachusetts, in connection with the 1889 General Convention. The YPCU's stated goal was "to promote an earnest Christian life among the young people of the Universalist Church, and the sympathetic union of all young people's societies, in their efforts to make themselves more useful in the service of God."

By 1892 there were 222 local groups in the national organization, with a total membership of approximately 9,000. When the YPCU held its 1893 meeting in Washington, DC, it had grown so important that its delegates were invited to a reception at the White House, where President Grover Cleveland shook hands with each of them. The YPCU, which considered itself more religious than social and a loyal and integral part of the denomination, was involved in missionary work almost from its founding, raising funds to establish new churches in the South and helping start a Post Office Mission to distribute Universalist literature. The youth were encouraged in these efforts by Quillen H. Shinn, who was just beginning his work as an itinerant missionary and had "swept into the YPCU orbit like a 'benevolent conflagration.' " In later years the priorities of the YPCU changed somewhat, but the organization remained an important part of the denomination and of its members' lives.

Another illustration of the trend toward greater organization was the founding during this period of an effective denominational women's association; it, too, has survived (and for the most part flourished) down to the present day, currently as the Unitarian Universalist Women's Federation. Established in 1869 as the Women's Centenary Aid Association to raise money for the centennial celebration, the organization was so successful (in less than two years it raised $35,000 and attracted 13,000 members) that in 1871 the members decided to remain in existence as the Women's Centenary Association, or WCA. It was subsequently renamed the Women's National Missionary Association in 1905, then the Association of Universalist Women in 1939, before merging with the Unitarian Women's Alliance in 1963.

Tension quickly developed between the WCA and the General Convention over the relationship between the two bodies—the WCA wished to retain its autonomy to avoid being dominated by the General Convention, and the General Convention did not want to see its work duplicated and diluted by that of the WCA. In a compromise reached in 1874, whereby the General Convention acknowledged the equal rights of women in all aspects of Universalist affairs, the WCA was made an integral part of the General Convention, and the leaders of the two bodies agreed to consult each other before undertaking any special projects.

The general purpose of the WCA was to promote "the interest of the Universalist Church"; its specific purposes were "to assist weak parishes, foster Sunday schools, help educate worthy young students for the ministry, relieve the needs of disabled preachers, ministers' wives and orphans, distribute denominational literature, and to do both home and foreign missionary work." Under the strong leadership of Caroline Soule, an extremely competent laywoman who served the group as president for eleven years before being ordained to the ministry, the WCA began working in all these areas. Members raised money to erect a women's dormitory at Lombard University and to endow a professorial chair at Buchtel College; they sent out missionaries, not only throughout the South and West, but also to Canada and Scotland; and they erected a memorial church at Murray Grove, near the spot where John Murray had first met Thomas Potter in 1770—these are but a few examples of the WCA's accomplishments. The emergence of laywomen as an organized force in the denomination was one of the most positive developments in this period of Universalist history; it would continue to energize the denomination in the years ahead.

Closely linked to the WCA's emergence as a force in the denomination were the continuing involvement of Universalists in the women's rights movement and the increasing numbers of women in the Universalist ministry. By 1892 some forty women had been ordained to the Universalist ministry, several of them serving in co-ministries with their husbands. Not surprisingly, a number of these women ministers, including Olympia Brown and Augusta Chapin, actively supported women's rights, especially the right to vote. In the last four decades of the century, Chapin, who had been ordained only a few months after Brown and had played a prominent role at the centennial observance, was a tireless reformer and missionary, mostly in the Midwest. Brown left the active ministry in 1887 (she was then fifty-two) in order to devote her full energies to securing the franchise for women; she lived to see her work rewarded by the ratification of the 19th Amendment in 1920. Mary Livermore, probably the most influential Universalist laywoman of her time, worked hard after the Civil War for women's rights and temperance. In addition to being one of the most popular lecturers on the lyceum circuit, she found time to serve as president of three important reform organizations: the Association for the Advancement of Women, the American Woman Suffrage Association, and the Massachusetts Woman's Christian Temperance Union.

Both Brown and Livermore were aided by husbands who strongly supported their work, as did many other men in the denomination, among them Horace Greeley, P. T. Barnum (a member of Brown's congregation in Bridgeport, Connecticut), and John Wesley Henley, a Midwestern minister who, as his name suggests, had converted from Methodism. Henley, who for a time served as chaplain of the National Woman Suffrage Association, persisted in pointing out that two large groups were denied freedom in America—African American men, and women regardless of color. Some men, however, and doubtless some women, were less supportive, especially of women in the ministry; it would be another century before the prejudice against women ministers was largely overcome.

With the passing on of older leaders, there was an inevitable shift in both emphasis and leadership, and much of the leadership in social reform passed into the hands of women. Hosea Ballou 2nd and Thomas Whittemore had both died in 1861, Charles Spear in 1863. Then, soon after the centennial, the denomination lost one of its most influential reformers when Democratic presidential nominee, Horace Greeley, died in 1872 shortly after his crushing defeat at the hands of Republican Ulysses S. Grant. Yet another leading reformer, Edwin Chapin, minister of the Fourth Universalist Society in New York City for over thirty years, died in 1880.

Although women's rights and temperance stood out as the major Universalist social concerns during this period, there were

In 1863, Olympia Brown (1835-1926) was the first woman minister in America to be ordained with full denominational authority.

The second Universalist woman to be ordained in 1863, Augusta Jane Chapin (1836-1905) was also the first woman in America to receive an honorary Doctor of Divinity degree.

others as well. In 1882 the General Convention unanimously passed a resolution, submitted by George Quinby of Maine, calling for the abolition of the death penalty; in 1883 the convention, out of concern over the rising divorce rate, called for the enactment of just and uniform divorce laws and reaffirmed the sanctity of marriage and "the supreme importance of the home as the safeguard of our national and religious life"; in 1884 the convention proclaimed "its world-wide sympathy with poor, unfortunate, struggling humanity" and called on Universalists to cooperate "with all movements and purposes for the prevention of cruelty to children and animals," and to work to remove the root causes of this cruelty.

Organized missionary work by Universalists, begun at the time of the centennial and well established by the early 1890s, marked yet another break with the denomination's past. To be sure, itinerant preachers like Nathaniel Stacy, George Rogers, and John Murray had been active in missionary work from the beginning; but that had been done on an *ad hoc* basis, as individual preachers had been moved to "go out on the highways and by-ways" to "give the people, not hell, but hope and courage." This new missionary activity was different. In one sense, it was the Universalists' response to what they perceived as their "coming of age"—the kind of enterprise that any established, self-respecting denomination would necessarily engage in; in another sense, it can be seen as an attempt to reclaim theological ground that other denominations had begun to invade, and which, if not reclaimed, would leave the Universalists with no place to stand.

But whatever their reason, after the centennial celebration Universalists were, as a body, committed to a strong organized missionary effort. Though much of the support for this effort initially came from the women's and youth organizations, the actual missionary work was done, as it had been done before, by individual ministers who were moved to forsake the comfort and security of a long-term settlement in an established parish and go afield to win converts to Universalism. The decision of the Women's Centenary Aid Association to continue in existence (as the Women's Centenary Association) after the centennial was a key factor in making the missionary movement possible, largely because the WCA returned a portion of its membership dues to the state from which the money had been collected to support the work of missionaries. As a result, many new churches were helped get a start in life, and others, established but struggling, managed to keep going.

While most of this missionary effort was carried on in the United States, particularly in the South and Midwest, it also, as noted earlier, extended into Canada and even overseas. In 1874 the WCA had received a plea for financial help from Universalists in Scotland, where six small societies had recently organized themselves into an association. A spokesperson for the societies described their situation as "precisely the same as it was in America about fifty years ago." In response, the WCA agreed to establish a Scottish mission and quickly mounted a drive to raise the necessary funds. When Caroline Soule, the WCA president, visited the Scottish Universalists the following year, she was impressed by the depth of their commitment but found them seriously handicapped by a lack of leadership and money.

Soon after her return, when the Scottish Universalists asked the WCA to provide a missionary for two years, Soule agreed to serve in that capacity herself. Enthusiastically received, she worked hard to put the movement on a sounder organizational basis by concentrating its efforts in a few areas rather than continuing to spread itself too thinly. Soule, who made her headquarters in Glasgow, preached several times each Sunday, regularly visited the outlying churches, organized what the Scots called "the American woman's Sunday school," and established a library of denominational materials donated, for the most part, by American Universalists. She also helped overcome, at least in part, the Scottish aversions to singing hymns and to Christmas celebrations, which they had previously dismissed as a popish practice. Before returning to America in 1880, at the end of her two years of service, Soule was ordained to the ministry by the Scottish Universalist Convention. She was replaced in Scotland by two male missionaries, but the delays between their appointments and the controversy between the WCA and General Convention over the worthiness of the Scottish mission caused much of the momentum behind the mission to be lost.

Finally, in 1886, Soule was persuaded to return to Glasgow, where she revitalized the mission and served the Scottish Universalists with distinction until her retirement in 1892. Scotland had become home for Soule, and she stayed until her death in 1903, at the age of seventy-nine. After her retirement the Scottish mission soon disintegrated and with it the Scottish Universalist movement.

One small church in Larbert managed to survive under lay leadership; in 1910 it affiliated with the Scottish Unitarian Association, with the proviso that it retain the Universalist name.

A few years before Soule retired, American Universalists embarked on another foreign mission, this time in Japan. Unlike the Scottish mission, which had been organized and funded mostly by the WCA, the mission to Japan was a project of the General Convention, although the WCA also contributed to its financial support. The idea of a Universalist mission to a non-Christian country had been discussed for almost a decade and became a reality in April 1890, when George Perin, Isaac Wallace Cate, and Margaret Schouler landed at Yokohama to begin their work. The mission's leader, Perin, had served successfully as minister of several Universalist churches; Cate had been a student at the Tufts Divinity School when he was recruited; Schouler, a member of Perin's Shawmut Avenue Church in Boston, was a teacher, musician, and painter. Before they left for Japan, Cate was ordained by the General Convention rather than the Massachusetts State Convention, a break with precedent signifying that his ministry would be in the name of the entire denomination.

The trio went to work in Tokyo as soon as they arrived, Cate and Schouler as English teachers, Perin as the overseer in constructing a combined church and mission headquarters. The building was dedicated on Christmas Day, 1890, and regular Sunday services began early in 1891, with an average attendance of sixty. Perin, understanding that Japanese ministers had to be trained if he wanted the mission to succeed, soon opened a theological school, even though at the start there were only two students, both converts to Universalism from orthodox Christianity. As an instructor of future ministers, Perin took pains to distinguish Universalist philosophy from that of other Christian denominations: "We shall not begin our work by trying to make these intelligent Japanese believe that their ancestors are now in hell for the simple reason that we did not come along a little sooner. I shall try to present the love of God . . . and to let hell take care of itself." By 1892 the number of students in the theological school had grown to seven; a "School of Liberal English" had been established, with an attendance of up to forty; tracts were being translated into Japanese and distributed; publication of a monthly newspaper had begun; financial support continued to come in from America. All in all, the Japan mission was off to a good start.

Meanwhile, as the Scottish mission was ending and the Japan mission beginning, a "one man missionary army" in the person of Quillen Shinn was beginning to make an impact on the domestic scene. Shinn, who had grown up in West Virginia, far from any Universalist church, had been converted to Universalism through the writings of George Quinby, the Maine editor and reformer, and Thomas Thayer, the leading Universalist theologian of the mid-nineteenth century. In 1867, having still had no personal contact with Universalists, he decided to go to the theological school at St. Lawrence and prepare for the ministry.

On the way Shinn stopped at Baltimore to attend the sessions of the General Convention and was so upset by the antagonistic quibbling that was going on over the Winchester Profession that, even though he was a newcomer without delegate status, he took the floor to express his dismay. Reportedly, he said that he had discovered that "Universalist ministers could write better than they could talk" and that after hearing them he wasn't sure he wanted to enter the ministry after all. His words were so powerful that what was later described as the "Baltimore bedlam" quickly changed into a "love feast," and Shinn was persuaded to continue with his original plan. After graduation and ordination he served a succession of parishes from 1870 until 1891 and then went on the road as a self-supported missionary of Universalism. An energetic, personable, self-confident man, Shinn, like Soule, was a good organizer, an effective fund raiser, and a strong preacher of Bible-based sermons. He would continue his missionary work for the next sixteen years, traveling the length and breadth of the country.

Another noteworthy missionary who began his work at this time was Joseph Jordan, the first African American person to be ordained to the Universalist ministry. Jordan was a native of Norfolk, Virginia, and, like Shinn, he had read his way to Universalism. Later, on a visit to Philadelphia, he joined the Church of the Messiah after hearing its minister, Edwin Sweetser, preach. Returning to Norfolk, Jordan quickly established a mission church there, and in 1889 the General Convention admitted the church to fellowship, ordaining Jordan at the same time. By 1891, with the help of an assistant, he had added both a Sunday school and a day school to his mission. Later, Jordan got financial support from both the Convention and the WCA and direct help from Shinn.

In addition to its missionary activities, the denomination showed other signs of maturation during this postcentennial period. All its colleges, except Buchtel, were becoming well established; scholars like Thomas Thayer, Richard Eddy, and Orello Cone were making their mark in theology, church history, and biblical studies; the Universalist Publishing House was growing into an important denominational press; summer institutes had been inaugurated on Cape Cod, at The Weirs on Lake Winnipesaukee in New Hampshire, at Ferry Beach on the Maine coast, and at Murray Grove, the site of John Murray's meeting with Thomas Potter on the Jersey shore.

At the same time, however, the attempt that had been made at the centennial convention to strengthen the denominational organization had not achieved the desired results. The hierarchical, three-tiered structure of General Convention, state conventions, and local parishes had largely failed to provide a framework for effective cooperation. The General Convention, without any significant administrative function or paid staff, was incapable of providing leadership; the state conventions were reluctant to give up their power to the General Convention; and the parishes, in turn, were reluctant to give up their power to the state conventions. At the heart of the problem was the individualism of most of the Universalists. Universalists have never been particularly disposed to surrendering their freedom to external authority, ecclesiastical or otherwise, and while they may have moved in the direction of denominational organization, they had not moved very far. Moreover, as the denomination approached its hundredth birthday, it was increasingly anxious about its future. The statistics were not encouraging; in 1890 the denomination had only 45,000 members, about óne in every 400 Protestants in the country. Just a half century earlier, Universalists had proudly claimed a constituency of several hundred thousand and their denomination to be the fifth or sixth largest in America.

While it was clear in retrospect that those earlier claims were greatly exaggerated, the Universalists in 1890 were forced to accept the reality that, whatever they may have been—or claimed to be—in the past, they were now a small denomination and barely holding their own, if that. Even more alarming was the growing realization that, despite their new missionary efforts, their *raison d'être* as a denomination was slowly fading away. "Hell was no longer a burning issue" for many Americans; an increasing number of mainline preachers had simply stopped stoking its fires. To some Universalists, the very survival of the denomination seemed threatened.

Chapter Six

"Improve the Property or Move Off the Premises"

The Struggle Back to Liberalism, 1893 –1918

The year 1893 came and went with no apparent recognition on the part of Universalists that it was the centennial of their existence as a denomination. Perhaps this was due to a disagreement about when the denomination had actually started. Some Universalists doubtless still contended that the association organized at Oxford, Massachusetts, in 1785 marked the beginning, even though the denominational historian, Richard Eddy, had recently made a convincing case for the later date, concluding that the Oxford Association had not survived past 1787. At any rate, whether it was disagreement, indifference, or more pressing business, the year passed with no celebration of the denomination's hundredth birthday.

An important event that could well have diverted Universalists' attention was the first World's Parliament of Religions, held in Chicago in September 1893 as part of the World's Columbian Exposition, or the Chicago World's Fair, as it was generally called. The parliament was one of the high points of the entire exposition, attracting representatives of almost every known religious faith, sect, and denomination in the world. It was properly termed "the greatest religious event of the nineteenth century," with an estimated 150,000 people attending during its seventeen days.

Universalist participation in the parliament was limited but significant. Augusta Chapin, who had been appointed chair of the Women's Committee, spoke at the opening session, pointing out that had the parliament "been called even one generation ago, it

must have lacked the cooperation and the presence in its delibera-
tion of one-half of the religious world." "Woman," she contended,
"could not have had a part in it . . . for two reasons: one, that her
presence would not have been thought of or tolerated; another,
that she herself was too weak to attempt, too unskilled to have
availed herself of the privilege . . . had it been extended to her." In
closing, she asked her audience to share the prophetic vision of
Isabella of Spain, who "beheld not only a new world, but also a new
future—an emancipated and intelligent womanhood and a
strengthened vision to bless the world." It was an emotional session,
punctuated with loud applause, the waving of handkerchiefs, and
"the mingling of tears and smiles."

Other Universalist speakers at the parliament were Everett
Rexford, a minister from Roxbury, Massachusetts, who spoke on
"The Religious Intent"; Mary Livermore, who gave a stirring ad-
dress on "The Religious Reunion of Christendom"; and Olympia
Brown, who presented a paper titled "Crime and Its Remedy." Both
Chapin and Brown made brief remarks at the closing session:
Chapin said that the parliament had been "the fulfillment of a
dream, the fulfillment of a long cherished prophecy," and Brown
asked her audience, "If ye love not your brother whom ye have
seen, how can ye love God whom ye have not seen?"

During the first five days of the parliament, Universalists (like
members of many other denominations) were holding a congress of
their own. More than twenty papers were presented by such denominational leaders as Brown, Rexford, Edwin Sweetser, A. A.
Miner, Isaac Atwood of St. Lawrence, and E. H. Capen of Tufts; a
paper by George Perin, the missionary to Japan, was read in his
absence. Attendance was high, with fifty-five ministers and hundreds of laypeople present for all or part of the congress. It was the
most significant Universalist gathering in terms of scholarly and
theological content since the centennial celebration nearly a quarter of a century earlier. Taken together, the parliament and congress provided Universalists with a fresh perspective on their
place in the global religious community and a larger vision of what
their faith might yet become.

An almost immediate result of the parliament was the formation a
year later of the American Congress of Liberal Religious Societies,
usually referred to in its early years as the Liberal Congress, and later
simply as "the congress." It had been founded "to unite in a larger
fellowship and cooperation, such existing societies and liberal ele-

ments as are in sympathy with the movement toward undogmatic religion; . . . to develop the church of humanity, democratic in organization, progressive in spirit, . . . cherishing the spiritual traditions and experiences of the past, but keeping itself open to all new light and the higher developments of the future." Of the more than 200 people who attended the organizational meeting, held in Chicago at Sinai Temple, over twenty were Universalist ministers.

Much of the support for the congress came from Chicago; by 1895 seventeen societies from the immediate area had affiliated: six Universalist and three Unitarian churches, three Jewish congregations, the Ethical Culture Society, a Quaker meeting, the Independent Liberal Church, the People's Church, and Jenkin Lloyd Jones's All Souls Church. By this time a progressive wing was beginning to emerge in Universalism, chiefly in the Midwest, which advocated a "New Universalism" that rejected narrow sectarianism and called for closer relations with other religious liberals; predictably, this wing gave the congress strong support. Also predictably, conservative Universalists viewed the congress with suspicion, if not outright hostility. The denominational press in particular strongly opposed the Liberal Congress, seeing it as a divisive force that threatened to undermine the denomination's Christian foundations. Nevertheless, while most Universalists evidently supported their press's position, many Universalist ministers either belonged to the congress or sympathized with its aims.

One of those most actively involved was A. N. Alcott, minister of the church in Elgin, Illinois, who was granted a year's leave of absence by his congregation to serve as the congress's secretary and missionary. Once Alcott had assumed his new position, the Illinois State Convention suspended his fellowship on the grounds that he was providing "professional services to a religious organization not in fellowship with the Universalist denomination." Alcott, who had the firm support of the Elgin church, strongly protested the convention's decision as both unfair and unconstitutional; the congress was not a denomination, he correctly maintained, and his work with it should be seen in the same light as if he had taken a temporary position with an organization like the YMCA. When the state convention refused to reverse itself, Alcott appealed to the General Convention; his case was referred to the Committee on Fellowship and Discipline but was never reported out. Undaunted, Alcott declared himself to be a Universalist minister who was no longer under ecclesiastical authority and continued his work with the congress. His case, which received wide attention, underscored the growing rift between the emerging liberal wing and the denomination's conservatives.

The second annual meeting of the Liberal Congress was, like the first, held at Sinai Temple in Chicago. Invitations had been sent to the Universalist state conventions and the General Convention, but most of the Universalists who attended were delegates from nearby churches. Undoubtedly in response to the light attendance by leaders of the denomination, J. M. Pullman, who had traveled to Chicago from Lynn, Massachusetts, and who served as spokesperson for the Universalists, repeated an oft-quoted challenge, variously attributed: "You Universalists," he said, "have squatted on the biggest word in the English language. Now the world is beginning to want that big word, and you Universalists must either improve the property or move off the premises!"

Universalists were to challenge themselves with these words for at least the next half century. The congress remained a viable organization for several years, but after 1900 it faded slowly away, its purposes having grown too vague to inspire commitment. As the new century began, however, other liberal interdenominational and interfaith organizations, both national and international, would enlist Universalist participation.

Meanwhile, the creed issue would not go away, even though many Universalists were heartily tired of hearing about it, much less discussing it. In 1893 the General Convention committee appointed to address the problem submitted another substitute statement to replace the Winchester Profession, but action on the report was deferred until the next convention. When the delegates convened again in 1895 (biennials had by then replaced annual meetings), something unexpected happened: the delegates accepted the committee's statement with only a few revisions by a vote of 69 to 15. The proposed new profession, on which an affirming vote was required at the next General Convention, read:

1. We believe in the universal Fatherhood of God and the universal Brotherhood of Man.

2. We believe that God, who has spoken through all His holy prophets since the world began, hath spoken to us

by His Son, Jesus Christ, our Example and Savior.

3. We believe that Salvation consists in spiritual oneness with God, who, through Christ, will finally gather in one the whole family of mankind.

The unexpected turn of events touched off a heavy, ongoing debate for the next two years. Some favored the new statement, others had alternative statements to propose, and still others insisted that the Winchester Profession be retained in its original form—after all, when it was adopted in 1803, it had been with the understanding that it would never be altered! Understandably, when the 124 delegates to the 1897 General Convention assembled in Chicago, the creed question was uppermost in their minds. After lively debate, the question was called on whether to adopt the proposed new profession; it went down in defeat by a vote of 102 to 1, the single vote in its favor being cast by Edwin Sweetser, one of its authors. The delegates then considered at length how the issue might be settled once and for all. Finally, a compromise plan was adopted by a vote of 94 to 30 whereby the General Convention's constitution would be amended as follows:

"Creed and Conditions of Fellowship"

1. The Profession of Faith adopted by this body at its session at Winchester, N.H., A.D. 1803, is as follows: [Here are the words of the original Profession.]

2. The conditions of fellowship in this Convention shall be as follows:

   I. The acceptance of the essential principles of the Universalist faith, to wit: The Universal Fatherhood of God; the spiritual authority and leadership of His Son, Jesus Christ; the trustworthiness of the Bible as containing a revelation from God; the certainty of just retribution for sin; the final harmony of all souls with God. The Winchester Profession is commended as containing these principles, but neither this, nor any other precise form of words, is required as a condition of fellowship, provided always that the principles above stated be professed.

II. The acknowledgement of the authority of the General Convention and assent to its laws.

The next General Convention, held in 1899 in Boston, was a milestone for the denomination. Not only did the attendance surpass that of the centennial, but the delegates showed a spirit of enthusiasm and cooperation that had been missing for some time from denominational affairs. The passage of the constitutional amendment was almost anti-climactic; it was ratified by a wide margin without debate. The delegates wanted to leave the matter behind them, and the compromise had something in it for almost everyone: the Winchester Profession was there for those who wanted it; there was a short list of principles for those who wanted a brief, modern statement of belief; and to the satisfaction of the vast majority, the Liberty Clause had been reinstated in fresh language. True, some delegates were not quite sure about the meaning of the phrase "provided always that the principles above stated be professed" (it was deleted in 1953), but this seemed unimportant at the time—this statement was accepted as a reassertion, however vague, of the individual right of conscience. Some outside the denomination may have been confused about the amendment's meaning, but the Universalists were simply relieved that they at long last had found a statement they could live with. The list of five principles, known as the Boston Declaration, soon came into wide use in the denomination as a general summary of Universalist beliefs. More important, the Liberty Clause that was attached to it meant there would be no further Universalist heresy trials.

The World's Parliament of Religions, the Liberal Congress, and the restoration of the Liberty Clause combined to bring the Universalists and the Unitarians closer together as the nineteenth century ended. Samuel Eliot, secretary of the American Unitarian Association (AUA), suggested in his 1899 annual report that "the time has come for a closer and more cordial cooperation with our brethren of the Universalist fellowship," and the General Convention was invited that year to join the AUA in appointing a committee to consider how such cooperation might best be achieved. The invitation was accepted by a vote of 101 to 26 over the strenuous objections of Sweetser, who had succeeded Thomas Whittemore as the denomination's leading opponent of any relationship with

Unitarians.

The joint committee, at its first meeting the following year, made it clear that it was "not desiring or expecting to disturb in any way the separate organic autonomy of the two denominations," as had been implied by the secular press. The committee's goal was "cooperation, not consolidation; unity, not union." Many Universalists, though not outspokenly critical of the committee, nevertheless had reservations; they saw the Unitarians as having drifted too far out of the Christian fold. As a result, the responsibilities of the committee ended up being quite narrowly defined; it was to deal only with those situations in which there might be friction between the two denominations, or a conflict of interest, or possible duplication of missionary efforts. In spite of these restrictions the joint committee continued to meet until 1907, but it never accomplished anything of major importance. Though the relationship between the two denominations was not damaged by the experiment, the gap between them remained too wide to be effectively bridged.

Beginning in 1905, however, the General Convention and the AUA began to cooperate closely as members of the International Congress of Religious Liberals, an organization that survives today as the International Association for Religious Freedom (IARF). Together, they hosted a highly successful conference in Boston that attracted 7,000 people from fifteen countries and more than thirty denominations and faiths. For Universalists in the early years of the twentieth century, working with Unitarians on the international level was evidently less threatening than on the continental level. Renewed talk about close cooperation between the two denominations on the continental level would not come for another twenty years.

The history of the Japan mission illustrates that there was ambivalence about cooperating with Unitarians even on the international level. When George Perin, I. W. Cate, and Margaret Schouler arrived in Japan in 1890, they were greeted warmly by Arthur Knapp, the Unitarian missionary who had arrived there a year earlier. Soon, they were working so closely with two other Unitarian missionaries, W. I. Laurence and Clay MacCauley, that Perin recommended the two denominations join forces and create a single mission. When Frank Oliver Hall (who was about to begin his long and distinguished ministry in New York City) offered a resolution to this effect at the 1891 General Convention, he even suggested that an eventual merger of the two denominations might have its beginning in Japan. This may well have been a tactical error, however, because numerous objections were immediately raised and the resolution failed. A. A. Miner spoke for many when he called the proposal "absurd and preposterous." The missionaries, however, continued to cooperate on a personal and informal basis.

Despite a small staff, inadequate funding, a formidable language barrier, the hostility of other missionaries, and a devastating earthquake, the Universalist mission to Japan remained in operation until the Second World War. But even in the early years, given the size of the staff and the level of financial support, the undertaking proved to be overly ambitious. The theological school had to close in 1900, after having graduated a total of eight students in its ten-year history. At one point in the early 1900s the missionaries even tried to set up twelve mission stations spread out over six hundred miles on three of the four main Japanese islands. When this proved unrealistic, they concentrated on strengthening the churches and schools at Tokyo, Shizuoka, and Nagoya, all in the central part of Honshu, Japan's most important island. At the same time, they encouraged Japanese Universalists wishing to prepare for the ministry to enroll at either Tufts or St. Lawrence.

One of the major accomplishments of the mission was the founding of the Blackmer Home in Tokyo, a place where Japanese girls could live in a supportive environment while pursuing an education, an undertaking not encouraged in prewar Japan. The home, which was established in 1903, continued in operation until the Second World War.

After the war, no official connection remained between the denomination and the Japanese Universalists (who numbered a thousand, at most), and no one seriously tried to reestablish the mission; the time for such enterprises had passed for the Universalists. Nevertheless, the Universalist Service Committee and the Association of Universalist Women helped the Japanese Universalists in several ways, including the building of the Koishikawa Universalist Center in Tokyo on the former site of the Blackmer Home. The Universalist Church of Japan, which in 1954 became a member of the Japan Free Religious Association, still teaches a traditional Universalist message. Thus, a century after the three American missionaries landed at Yokohama, Universalism survives in Japan, albeit on a small scale, as a Japanese enterprise. Despite its limited scope, the Japan mission was, in Russell Miller's words, "indeed, an 'investment in Universal Brotherhood' of which Universalists could justifiably be proud."

On the domestic front, the mission that Joseph Jordan began in Norfolk, Virginia, in the late 1880s became better established over time. In 1893 Edwin Sweetser arranged for Jordan to address the General Convention in Washington, DC, on the subject "Our Mission to the Colored People"; his plea for support raised enough money to build a small chapel in connection with his mission. The new building was dedicated as the First Universalist Church of Norfolk (Huntersville Section) the following year, with Sweetser preaching the principal sermon.

Both the church and the school grew rapidly, and in 1898 a second mission was organized in Suffolk, about twenty miles away, and placed in the charge of Thomas Wise, a recently fellowshiped minister whom Jordan had converted to Universalism. The mission, which ministered to the families of workers at the local Planters Peanut factory, immediately began to thrive under Wise's leadership. Unfortunately, with the two operations going well, Jordan died in 1901, and Wise, who then had taken charge of both missions, soon left to become a Methodist. While the Norfolk mission never recovered from this loss of leadership and gradually faded out of existence, the Suffolk mission fared better.

In 1904 Joseph Fletcher Jordan, another African American convert to Universalism (not related to the other Joseph Jordan), came to head the Suffolk mission and stayed until his death twenty-five years later. Jordan had been inspired to enter the ministry by Quillen Shinn, who arranged for him to study at the St. Lawrence Theological School for a year before coming to Suffolk; he was granted fellowship soon after his arrival. Under Jordan's leadership, the mission, which had virtually ceased operations after Wise departed, made a remarkable recovery; within a few years the day school's enrollment had risen from "almost nothing" to 186, and the church's membership from one (Wise had taken some of the members with him) to twenty-three, with fifty families in the parish. Jordan was an extremely versatile man who enjoyed good relationships with whites as well as African Americans. For a time, in addition to his work at the mission, he served as parole officer for some 700 youths. (It was said that no one who attended his school had ever been arrested—a backhanded compliment, but given the realities of life in Suffolk, a real tribute to his work.)

Jordan also served as a correspondent for two periodicals and published one himself, the *Colored Universalist*. The Suffolk mission, which, aside from its religious activities, provided a practical education to hundreds of African Americans with its day school and night courses, remained an important force for social change throughout Jordan's lifetime. After his death the church ceased to function, but the school continued under the leadership of his daughter, Annie B. Willis.

Eventually, the school, still with significant Universalist support, evolved into a combined day-care center, nursery school, and community center known as the Jordan Neighborhood House. After the Unitarian-Universalist merger in 1961, the Unitarian Universalist Service Committee became the denominational link, but in 1969, for reasons that were never adequately explained, the committee withdrew its support, an action that still upsets many from the Universalist side of the merger. By the time of Mrs. Willis's death in 1977, the preschool program had been taken over by the Southeastern Tidewater Opportunity Project, and the Neighborhood House had become the Jordan Community Center, with only the Jordan name to link it to the past.

About 400 miles west of Suffolk, in the Blue Ridge Mountains of North Carolina, there existed in the first half of the twentieth century yet another Universalist home mission. Known as Inman's Chapel and set in the isolated Pigeon River Valley far from towns, cities, or even paved roads, the mission had roots stretching back to the 1860s, when an itinerant preacher came through the valley and converted some of its people to Universalism. A church was soon organized, and the small congregation ordained one of its own, James Anderson Inman, a farmer, as its settled minister. He served the church as preacher for forty-five years, almost until his death at the age of eighty-seven. For many years services were held in members' homes, but in 1902 Quillen Shinn visited the valley and encouraged the congregation to erect a chapel. With pledges of $4 in cash and eighty hours in labor, construction was started, and both Shinn and Inman helped with the work. The building was dedicated by Shinn the following year as Inman's Chapel, in honor of its seventy-seven-year-old minister.

After Inman's death in 1913, the Women's National Missionary Association (WNMA), which had assumed the responsibility of supporting denominational work in North Carolina, provided some financial help to Inman's Chapel and explored ways to expand its

Quillen Hamilton Shinn, Universalist missionary to the rural South in the 1890s, and Isaac Morgan Atwood, the first superintendent of the Universalist General Convention, at Ferry Beach Park.

program. Eventually, Hannah Jewett Powell, who had graduated from the theological school at Tufts in 1899 and had served with the Universalist Sea Coast Mission in Maine, went to Pigeon River as a missionary. Powell, who arrived in 1921 and stayed for fifteen years, not only soon revitalized the congregation but also established a thriving Sunday school, a kindergarten, a summer school, adult evening courses, and an infirmary. With help from the WNMA, a new building named Friendly House was erected to accommodate these activities.

Under Powell, who was termed "a whole social service organization" embodied in one woman, the mission became the spiritual, educational, and social center of the small, isolated mountain community. After Powell retired in 1936, George and Annie Boorn carried on the mission's work for the next seven years under the difficult conditions brought on by the depression and the war. In

1947, after several futile attempts to find new leadership, and after Powell herself came back for several months in an effort to revitalize the operation, the Pigeon River mission was finally abandoned; by then the need for such a mission had largely disappeared. The Inman's Chapel congregation continued to exist for another decade; then it too was gone. Still, both deserve to be remembered as a unique part of denominational history and as a witness to the extraordinary commitment of Inman, Powell, and many others.

Even without his involvement with the Suffolk and Pigeon River missions, Quillen Shinn would qualify as the denomination's most ambitious, energetic, and peripatetic missionary around the turn of the century. Suffolk and Pigeon River were but two of the literally hundreds of places that he visited and on which he left his mark during his sixteen years of missionary work. For the first four years of his travels he was both a self-appointed and self-supported missionary, but in 1895 the General Convention, impressed by his accomplishments, named him as its official "General Missionary" at an annual salary of $3,000.

It was money well spent; according to Shinn's first biennial report, he had visited thirty-four states, the District of Columbia, and two Canadian provinces; had organized eight churches, four state conferences, two state YPCUs, twenty-five local YPCUs, six Ladies' Aid societies, and three mission circles; had averaged almost one sermon or address a day, received 350 people into church membership, christened innumerable children, and traveled over 15,000 miles. Moreover, much of his time had been spent revisiting churches he had helped established earlier, when he was out on his own. He worked mostly in the rural South, but wherever he went, his pattern was much the same: he would search out a few Universalists, or at least people sympathetic to his views; advertise an open meeting; preach a sermon or two wherever he could find a place; and then, if possible, organize a congregation, solicit money for a building, identify and empower lay leadership, and be on his way again, planning to come back later to see how things were going and to give whatever help was needed.

In his new position, Shinn at first reported to the General Convention's trustees, who gave him more or less a free hand, but in 1898 the situation changed. The convention, feeling it needed a full-time paid executive, had established the position of General Superintendent and appointed Isaac M. Atwood, president of the theological school at St. Lawrence, to fill the office. Among other responsibilities, Atwood oversaw the convention's missionary work, an area in which he and Shinn had sharp differences of opinion. Atwood thought Shinn was spreading his efforts too thin and was establishing new churches without adequate ministerial leadership and in places where their survival seemed doubtful; he felt efforts should instead be concentrated in urban centers. Shinn, on the other hand, believed that churches should be organized in every corner of the country, no matter how remote, and that committed lay leaders, including lay preachers, were generally adequate to maintain them.

Despite his many supporters, Shinn seemed in jeopardy of losing his position, but in time a compromise was reached: Shinn agreed to confine his work to the South under the new title of Southern missionary, while Atwood assumed responsibility for the rest of the convention's missionary activities.

Shinn, a "Bible Universalist," also had sharp differences with the new breed of young ministers who identified themselves as liberals; he refused to identify Universalism as a liberal religion, believing liberalism was too closely identified with Unitarianism, which he characterized as the "go as you please church." But despite his theological conservatism, Shinn strongly advocated social reform, particularly prison reform and the abolition of the death penalty. When he learned that in a straw vote at a ministers' meeting, five out of a group of twenty-four had voted in favor of capital punishment, he termed it "the most mortifying thing I have read since I have been in the Universalist ministry."

Shinn died of rheumatic fever at his home in Medford, Massachusetts, in 1907 at the age of sixty-two, after a missionary trip to South Carolina. Not long before, during the two years of 1904 and 1905, he had reportedly traveled more than 38,000 miles, 900 of them on horseback or by foot. Russell Miller observes:

> There is no completely accurate way of measuring Shinn's permanent accomplishments . . . , but there is no question that he recruited hundreds of individuals, was responsible for building churches by the dozens (at least forty), and was responsible for almost thirty additions to the ministry. . . . [But] it was the spirit that was engendered by such persons as Shinn, and not the statistical evidence, that was ultimately important.

Although Shinn found strong support in the denomination for his views on prison reform and the abolition of the death penalty (beginning in 1899 the fourth Sunday in October was designated by the General Convention as Prison Sunday to encourage congregations to focus on these issues), the denomination had an unimpressive record of working for reform during this particular period. While people like Olympia Brown and Mary Livermore continued to work for women's suffrage and a few state conventions passed resolutions in its favor, the General Convention on several occasions between 1905 and 1911 either tabled or defeated resolutions on the subject, even though the 1874 convention had gone on record as supporting equal rights for women.

In the area of labor relations, Universalists also had difficulty in putting their theology into practice, as demonstrated by the notorious Pullman strike of 1894. George Pullman, a wealthy Universalist industrialist and brother of two Universalist ministers, having made his fortune by perfecting the "railroad palace sleeping car," had built a model industrial city south of Chicago to house his employees. With its many amenities, this city of 10,000 was touted as the result of ideal owner-worker relations. The idyll was shattered in 1894, however, after a severe economic depression had resulted in wage cuts and layoffs without a corresponding lowering of utility charges or rents for employee housing; moreover, Pullman left management salaries untouched and continued to pay dividends to his stockholders. After he rejected the workers' demands for relief and refused to submit their grievances to arbitration, 3,000 workers went on strike, forcing the plant to close. Federal troops were brought in to quell the resulting violence; the strike collapsed, leaving the workers worse off than before.

The Universalist press and many denominational leaders supported Pullman, though some voices cried in protest, including those of Orello Cone, the biblical scholar and author of *Rich and Poor in the New Testament*, and Levi Powers of Somerville, Massachusetts. Powers, contrasting the Republic of the United States with the Republic of God, observed that the former "believes that three thousand men should ask another man for the right to live and work—that those who come late should pay the children of those who come early for a chance to live on the footstool of the Most High, that some men have a right by law to compel others to contribute to their success." His was probably a minority opinion; most Universalists seemed content to stay in the capitalistic mainstream, favoring a benevolent paternalism toward industrial workers. When Pullman died in 1897, Charles Eaton, minister of the Church of the Divine Paternity in New York City, included the following in his memorial remarks to the General Convention:

> Democracy is not mobocracy; not the undermining of existing institutions. A false democracy has drunk of anarchism and law has been forgotten in the drivel of what is base. The Universalist church is the child of the people; [she] came up out of the soil, and industry has crowned her if she should be crowned at all.

Around the turn of the century, much of the energy that Universalists had earlier put into social reform was diverted to social service and benevolence in local communities. During this time, Universalists founded numerous institutions such as settlement houses, homes for orphans and children from broken families, homes for young women, and homes for the aging and infirm in cities like Minneapolis, Philadelphia, New York, and Boston. A number of them still exist today, including the Bethany Union for Young Women in Boston; the Doolittle Home for the retired in Foxboro, Massachusetts; and the Messiah Home for the elderly in Philadelphia, now merged with the Unitarians' Joseph Priestley House to form the Unitarian Universalist House of the Joseph Priestley District.

One unique undertaking was the establishment in 1894 of the Every Day Church, an outgrowth of the Shawmut Avenue Universalist Church in Boston. George Perin had served as minister of this church before going to Japan as a missionary. When he returned, he recognized a real need to expand church programs to meet the needs of the neighborhood. The congregation bought a large house next door to the church and used it as headquarters for day and evening classes in stenography, drawing, dressmaking, and cooking; a day nursery for the children of working mothers; and a legal aid center. The Every Day Church was an immediate success, and Perin recruited a large number of volunteers to staff its many programs. When the Shawmut Avenue church merged with the Brookline church a decade later, some of the activities of the Every Day Church were continued at the new site.

By 1911, however, the denomination was experiencing a resurgence of interest in social reform; the Social Gospel movement led by Walter Rauschenbusch had gotten under way, and Universalists were quick to join. The General Convention appointed a Commission on Social Service with Frank Oliver Hall as its chair to educate the denomination about the best ways of effecting social reform. Almost at once the General Convention was flooded with resolutions on such subjects as temperance, women's suffrage, scientific agriculture, and tax reform, and in support of innumerable charities; all were referred to the commission for study and advice. The 1913 General Convention was addressed by Rauschenbusch himself, and the 1915 Convention was addressed by Jane Addams of Chicago's Hull House. Several state commissions were organized, and local churches set up committees to hold forums on social issues. When war broke out in Europe, Levi Powers, the Commission's chief adviser, journeyed there to study firsthand the underlying economic causes.

The member of the Commission on Social Service who was to make the greatest impact in applying the Social Gospel to Universalism was its Secretary, Clarence Russell Skinner, who had been Hall's assistant in New York City before moving on to churches in Mount Vernon, New York, and Lowell, Massachusetts. A member of a distinguished Universalist family, he had entered the ministry without any formal seminary training immediately after graduating from St. Lawrence University. Skinner quickly gained a reputation for successfully applying Universalist social principles both to the churches he served and to the larger community, so when a position opened up on the Crane Theological School faculty at Tufts in 1914, he was offered and accepted an appointment as Professor of Applied Christianity.

Skinner, who would teach at Crane until his retirement thirty-one years later, is generally regarded as the greatest Universalist of the twentieth century, and it did not take him long to make his mark. In 1915 *The Social Implications of Universalism* appeared, a book in which Skinner interpreted the Social Gospel in global terms that went beyond traditional Christianity. Then, two years later, "A Declaration of Social Principles," written by Skinner on behalf of the commission, was adopted by the denomination as the basis for its social witness. The preamble to the declaration's working program stated that "through all the agencies of the church we shall endeavor to educate and inspire the community and the nation to a keener social consciousness and a truer vision of the kingdom of God on the earth."

Dean of Tufts University's Crane Theological School and co-founder of the non-denominational Community Church of Boston, Clarence Russell Skinner (1881-1949) was a prophet of the social gospel.

The declaration concluded with an outline of the program of the Universalist Church for "completing humanity." It called for the following:

> *First*: An Economic Order which shall give to every human being an equal share in the common gifts of God, and in addition all that he shall earn by his own labor.

> *Second*: A Social Order in which there shall be equal rights for all, special privileges for none, the help of the strong for the weak until the weak become strong.

> *Third*: A Moral Order in which all human law and action shall be an expression of the moral order of the universe.

> *Fourth*: A Spiritual Order which shall build out of the growing lives of living men the growing temple of the living God.

Skinner was a pacifist, and after the United States entered the First World War, many of his fellow clergy shunned him as a result. At one point his senior colleagues even grilled him at length on his views, suspecting that he might be a Marxist, a charge that Skinner flatly denied. Both Dean Lee McCollester of Crane and President John Cousens of Tufts staunchly defended Skinner, not because they shared his convictions but because they respected his integrity and were committed to freedom of speech.

When the war ended and Universalists could pause to take stock of their situation, they for the most part felt optimistic about the future. Although the number of their churches had decreased significantly during the last quarter century (only 679 had been reported in 1916 as compared with 801 in 1894), most of these losses involved small rural or village churches, and the denomination could take heart that total membership appeared (on the basis of admittedly unreliable statistics) to be holding its own. More important, the denomination had survived a theological controversy and reestablished the right to freedom of conscience. Moreover, it seemed to be moving beyond simple "no hellism" toward a broader theology and new global social ethic appropriate to the times. The property may have eroded a bit, but it had not been vacated, and improvements were seemingly under way.

Chapter Seven

"We Do Not Stand, We Move"

The Search for a New Identity, 1919–1944

Despite the optimism with which they entered it, the period between the two world wars proved to be difficult and wrenching for
many Universalists. Many members believed that the denomination had lost its purpose, and felt sad to see so many churches
slowly dying on the vine. Since Universalists are generally
optimistic, some of them felt that a revitalization of their faith lay
ahead, and others interpreted the decline as evidence that their
distinctive doctrine had carried the day, even if members of other
Protestant denominations would not admit it, and that their work
was over.

In retrospect, the decline was caused by three factors, one
sociological, one organizational, and one theological. Sociologically,
the migration of Americans to the cities and to the West left many
of the rural or village churches without the critical mass to sustain
them. Organizationally, the denomination remained crippled by
its distrust of centralized power and the resulting difficulty in
mounting unified action. Theologically and most important, the
Universalists had to confront such basic questions as whether
they, in fact, still had a unique, relevant doctrine to proclaim, and
whether they were moving, or should be moving, beyond the outer
limits of Christianity.

But, as George Huntston Williams has so perceptively recognized, there was a "deep sense nurtured in the heart of most
Universalists throughout . . . their history that they had a unique
mission as a church," and this sense of mission helped them
survive while they struggled to formulate a wider meaning for

their faith. Lewis B. Fisher, dean of the Ryder Divinity School in Chicago, put it this way in 1921: "Universalists are often asked to tell where they stand. The only true answer to give to this question is that we do not stand at all, we move." The question was, in what direction?

The denomination entered the postwar years with great expectations of entering a whole "new epoch." In connection with the sesquicentennial of John Murray's landing in America, a Million Dollar Campaign was launched in 1920 with the double slogan of "A Greater Universalist Church" and "A World Church for World Service."

Consecutive celebrations at Murray Grove and Gloucester commemorated the sesquicentennial year, and while neither was on the scale of the centennial observance, both attracted large turnouts and generated new enthusiasm. The Murray Grove celebration included conventions of both the Young People's Christian Union and the General Sunday School Association, as well as the dedication of the newly enlarged Murray Grove House, a hotel designed to accommodate church and denominational meetings. The celebration at Gloucester included a well-attended convention of the Laymen's League and a great pageant depicting John Murray's part in the beginnings of American Universalism. In addition, plans were announced for both a Murray Anniversary Crusade to double church membership and a fund drive to establish Gloucester as a national shrine and headquarters for annual meetings of the whole denomination.

Then the following year the General Convention announced plans for a "Christ Crusade" designed to reaffirm a commitment to universal brotherhood, the Golden Rule, and the Social Gospel of Jesus—all this to implement the Declaration of Social Principles authored by Clarence Skinner and adopted by the General Convention four years earlier.

During that same year the Women's National Missionary Association acquired title to the Clara Barton Homestead in Oxford, Massachusetts, dedicating it on Christmas Day, 1921, the hundredth anniversary of Barton's birth. (A highly successful camp for diabetic girls that was later established on the property remains a vital institution today.) All things considered, Universalists had every right to be optimistic as they entered their "new epoch."

Predictably, Clarence Skinner continued to emerge as a force for change in the denomination. In 1919 he had given an address at Boston's Faneuil Hall titled "America in Crisis," in which he praised a strike by the International Workers of the World in Centralia, Illinois, and denounced the members of the American Legion as "anarchists." So many people were upset by Skinner's words that the State Attorney General wrote to President John Cousens of Tufts, calling his attention to the matter, but Cousens remained firm in his support of Skinner's right to free speech.

The following year, Skinner and John Haynes Holmes established the Community Church of Boston, patterned after the non-denominational community church that resulted from Holmes's reorganization of the Unitarian Church of the Messiah in New York City. Skinner and Holmes had been drawn together by their theological and social liberalism and by their pacifism; both had evoked severe criticism for their stands on the war, and Holmes had even gone so far as to resign his Unitarian fellowship a few years earlier to protest the condemnation of pacifism by the General Conference of Unitarian Churches. Like its counterpart in New York, the Boston church was also nondenominational. Its members were required only to subscribe to a "bond of union" that called for mutual assistance and fellowship to promote "the cause of truth, righteousness, and love in the world." The church, which met in rented quarters, attracted large congregations almost from the start with its program of social action and its Sunday services of "rational worship" followed by a forum for free discussion. Skinner served as the church's "leader" (the traditional term of minister was not used) until 1936. Both the Boston and the New York churches survive as members of the Unitarian Universalist Association and are served by ministers in Unitarian Universalist fellowship.

Skinner's involvement with the Community Church undoubtedly upset conservative Universalists, as did his theology, which, though expressed in marginally Christian terms, was at heart a social action-oriented global humanism that stressed "a spiritual interpretation of the whole of life" that gave "insight into the unities and universals" of religion. For Skinner, a truly universal religion had to be "founded upon a twentieth century psychology and theology, a religion which is throbbing with the dynamics of democracy, a spirituality which expresses itself in terms of humanism, rather than in terms of individualism."

Although his theology went far beyond the limits of traditional Christianity, it did incorporate the main elements of the Protestant

Social Gospel: the immanence of God, an organic (or unified) view of the social order, the ethical teachings of Jesus, and the progressive establishment of the Kingdom of God on earth. Skinner particularly emphasized this last element, having begun his *Social Implications of Universalism* by stating, "How to transform this old earth into the Kingdom of Heaven—that's the primal question." Undoubtedly, this grounding in biblical principles helped make his theology acceptable to many conservative Universalists and allowed the denomination as a whole to support his social agenda; it went strongly on record in favor of United States membership in the League of Nations and endorsed treaties and conferences designed to promote international cooperation and world peace. Even Skinner's pacifism, which had been so vigorously attacked only a few years earlier, received endorsement via a General Convention resolution that recognized the right of individual Universalists "to follow the voice of conscience" with regard to participation in future wars.

Nevertheless, despite, or perhaps because of, these liberalizing trends, the denomination began to flounder badly. Many Universalists were unwilling or unable to move toward a new concept of Universalism, and even if they had, the denomination, with its emerging new understanding of itself, would probably not have attracted enough new members to replace those who were dying off.

Few village or rural churches survived the theological and sociological transformations that were taking place. In Madison County in upstate New York, for example, Universalist churches had been established during the nineteenth century in the villages and hamlets of Morrisville, Cazenovia, Sheds Corners, Hamilton, Madison, Lebanon, Erieville, and Stockbridge. Only two of these churches survived into the twentieth century, and by 1943 the last had disappeared. Today, it is difficult to imagine that such churches ever existed in these places, and while many of the churches in the larger towns and cities did survive and some even flourished, their support of denominational programs was limited, at best.

While the Million Dollar Campaign had been a qualified success, later attempts to raise money for the General Convention's programs failed, as did the Murray Anniversary and Christ Crusades designed to double membership in the denomination. Because of the members' confusion over the relationship between quotas, special projects, and capital fund drives, it was decided in 1929 to work out a careful, comprehensive plan for matching program to income; unfortunately, the stock market crash and the depression that followed made it impossible to carry out the plan and further weakened the denomination's fiscal position.

Bearing much of the burden and frustration of these failures were the General Superintendents who served during this period, John Smith Lowe (1917–1928) and Roger Etz (1928–1938), to whom the denomination had given major responsibility for carrying out programs but not the necessary resources in money and personnel. Etz, in particular, serving as he did during the bleak years of the depression, could do no more than carry on a holding operation.

The problem, however, went much deeper than inadequate financing. As Frank D. Adams put it in his 1929 presidential address to the General Convention, Universalists had seemingly lost their sense of mission, were overly concerned with what those in other denominations thought of them, and had surrounded themselves with an "impalpable wall of conservatism"; the very survival of the denomination was at stake, and he called on the clergy to be pioneers again, drawing on the legacy of freedom and courage they had inherited from the past. The address received mixed reviews; some thought it prophetic, while others were angered and muttered that Adams should not be reelected president. During the decade that followed, more and more voices would be raised in concern over the denomination's future.

One of the rare successes of the General Convention during this period was the founding of the Universalist National Memorial Church in Washington, DC, and the construction of its impressive building. In 1921 the convention proposed to establish a church that would memorialize Universalists who had served overseas in the Great War (and others who had "proved themselves worthy of a national memorial") and strengthen the denomination's base in the nation's capital. Objections to the proposal were raised on many grounds, particularly by Universalists in the Midwest, who saw the project as unnecessary and an inappropriate use of limited resources. However, by 1928 enough money had been raised so that construction could begin, and the building was completed two years later; the first service was held on Palm Sunday with a congregation of over 500 in attendance. The building cost almost half a million dollars, considerably more than originally expected, and this, along with the decrease in contributions caused by the depression, had forced the convention's trustees to take out a mortgage in order to complete the work.

Among those memorialized by the building were Owen D. Young, a prominent Universalist businessman and diplomat who had helped solve the war reparations problem, and John van Schaick, a minister who had served as Red Cross Commissioner to Belgium during the war and later as president of the District of Columbia Board of Education and editor of the *Universalist Leader*. Frederic Perkins, the church's minister from 1927 until 1938, oversaw the planning and erection of the building in the early years of his ministry and led a large and vigorous congregation after its completion. He was succeeded by Seth Brooks, whose tenure extended until 1979, and then by William Fox, who served the church for a decade, after which James Blair became the church's minister.

In addition to the difficulties of financing the National Memorial Church, the denomination felt the effects of the depression in many other ways. As mentioned earlier, Lombard College was forced out of existence, and the programs of the General Convention had to be drastically curtailed. In 1930 the convention's two most important offices, those of General Superintendent and General Secretary, had to be combined out of financial necessity; in 1932 Roger Etz, by then doing the work of both offices, voluntarily took a 10 percent cut in salary to help keep the convention in operation. The theological schools at St. Lawrence and Tufts limped along with very limited resources, as did many churches; still less fortunate churches were forced to close their doors forever. Shrinking incomes made it difficult for many churches to pay a minister's salary, and for women ministers, in particular, it was difficult to find placements. "There is a tremendous prejudice against women ministers," wrote General Superintendent Etz. "At the present time I find it practically impossible to get any woman minister a hearing at any salary whatever." Extension efforts also came to a virtual standstill; there was neither money nor a successor to Quillen Shinn who was willing to go out on the road as a missionary with no denominational support.

During this difficult period, the Universalists were courted by both the Unitarians and the Congregationalists, and both were open to the possibility of complete merger. The two denominations, without each other's knowledge, had sent resolutions to the 1925 General Convention proposing closer relationships, and for several years the special Universalist commission appointed to respond struggled with these twin overtures, one from the left, the other from the right. The commission worked with its Congregationalist counterpart to produce a highly publicized joint statement calling for closer cooperation between the two denominations; it was accepted by the 1927 General Convention, but the matter died when it became obvious that the Universalists were reluctant to move any further toward union. Behind this reluctance, concludes Russell Miller, "was the ever present and pervasive fear by Universalists that their identity would be irretrievably lost, and that the denomination and its traditions would cease to exist. Absorption by another denomination was too high a price to pay for whatever advantage there might be."

Samuel A. Eliot, the outgoing president of the American Unitarian Association, had been somewhat piqued by the Universalists' flirtation with the Congregationalists. In a long letter to John van Schaick, editor of the *Leader*, he stated that the Unitarian overture two years earlier had not been "a mere gesture," but if the Universalists preferred "to turn backward and fall in with the main body of the Christian army that is slowly and hesitantly coming along the roads that the Universalists and Unitarians had blazed, then the Unitarians will have to go ahead alone." When the Universalists had finished "making their polite bows to Orthodoxy," he wrote, the Unitarians would be glad to welcome them back, though they might well have some catching up to do.

The tone of the letter offended many Universalists, but nevertheless, the dialogue initiated by the Unitarian overture continued, and a joint commission was established in 1931. The commission outlined three alternatives: maintenance of the *status quo*, complete merger, or formation of a larger fellowship that would include *all* religious liberals in one great umbrella organization. The commission recommended the third of these options, having recognized that a basic, unbridgeable difference still existed between the views of freedom held by the two denominations: the Unitarians saw their freedom as unlimited, while the Universalists recognized that their freedom, while broad, was nevertheless restricted by their Statement of Belief, despite the Liberty Clause that went with it.

By 1933 both the American Unitarian Association and the General Convention had accepted the commission's recommendation, and the Free Church Fellowship (FCF) came into existence with the new AUA president, Louis Cornish, at its head. In order to secure Universalist approval the proposed preamble to the FCF constitution had to be amended to include a phrase about working "for the Kingdom of God in the spirit of Jesus." In order to encourage the broadest possible membership in the new organization, it was specified that four members of the governing council should be chosen from outside the Unitarian and Universalist ranks. Accordingly, three Congregationalists were chosen, along with John Haynes Holmes, minister of the independent Community Church of New York and a strong supporter of the undertaking.

With the organization established, at least on paper, the council began efforts to recruit member societies. The results were disappointing. Harry Emerson Fosdick, the leading liberal Baptist minister of the day, had no interest in "organizations at the top" that ended up wasting their time with "a lot of speech making"; the Hicksite Quakers were interested but feared their involvement would undercut their attempts to heal a longstanding breach with orthodox Quakers; the Ethical Culture Society was not interested, quite possibly because of the amendment to the preamble that the Universalists had insisted upon; and even the Congregationalists shied away, calling the whole undertaking "impractical."

In the spring of 1934, a mere twenty-one churches were voted into membership—nine Unitarian, nine Universalist, and three community churches. A year later, the total had risen to only eighty-one, representing but a tiny fraction of the potential membership. The Free Church Fellowship came to an ignominious end in 1937, a victim of lack of funds, members, definition, and interest. From the start there had been internal struggles between the Universalists and the Unitarians over the basic nature of the enterprise, and many thought the joint commission had made a mistake in recommending what they saw as a timid middle course rather than coming out strongly in favor of merger. Russell Miller explains the failure of the FCF in these words:

> It had been created as a half-way house which satisfied very few, as a step toward merger which the Unitarians were much more willing to push than were the Universalists. It had attempted both too little and too much, with resources which in no way matched the idealistic, not to say grandiose, plans for the future. The motive power had come from a small band of denominational leaders, without grass-roots support, to appeal to a larger

fellowship among religious liberals. Instead, it had become entangled with a continuing internal squabble between Universalists and Unitarians over their relationship. [Others] felt themselves to be outsiders who were witnessing a strictly family quarrel.

In spite of the demise of the FCF, the close though often strained relations between the two denominations made it inevitable that the Unitarians' "humanist controversy" of the 1920s and 1930s would spill over into the Universalist arena. At one level the controversy, which often grew heated, was merely a question of semantics; at another level it was a disagreement between naturalists and supernaturalists; and on yet another it was a disagreement between theists and nontheists. At the heart of the controversy was the question of whether humanity could control its own destiny. For a number of years the pages of Unitarian and Universalist periodicals were filled with a great variety of opinions on the subject.

A widely publicized "Humanist Manifesto" that appeared in 1933 spelled out a radical humanist position, claiming that a distinction could no longer be made between the sacred and the secular; that the universe was self-existing rather than created; and that traditional religion was no longer relevant. "Man," the manifesto declared, "is at last becoming aware that he alone is responsible for the realization of the world of his dreams, that he has within himself the power for its achievement." Thirty-four men signed the document (presumably no women were invited to do so), thirteen of them Unitarian ministers. Clinton Lee Scott, at that time minister in Peoria, Illinois, was the only Universalist signatory, although two of the Unitarian signers, J. A. C. Fagginer Auer and Charles Francis Potter, also held Universalist fellowship. While presumably all Universalists were at least somewhat humanistic, since they affirmed the inherent worth of all people and were committed to work for the betterment of society, most of them rejected the humanist label with its nontheistic and non-Christian implications. They did not, however, reject Scott; after the manifesto appeared, he was reelected as a trustee of the General Convention by "a sizeable margin."

Although most Universalists rejected radical departures in theology like the manifesto, by the late 1920s there was a growing sentiment in the denomination that the Boston Declaration of

1899 was no longer an adequate expression of the Universalist faith. New developments in biblical criticism and science, the Social Gospel movement, the impact of humanism (whether admitted to or not), and the influence of Clarence Skinner's theology all combined to make the previous statement seem dated and out of step with current thinking. Accordingly, a three-person committee, consisting of Frederic Perkins, John Murray Atwood, and Max Kapp, was appointed in 1931 to propose a new statement that would supplement the statements of 1803 and 1899. In sharp contrast to the long debates that preceded adoption of the Boston Declaration, the committee's recommendation was approved with few changes and no opposition, both preliminarily in 1933 and finally two years later. The new Bond of Fellowship and Statements of Faith (the added portion is usually referred to as the "Washington Avowal") read as follows:

> The bond of fellowship in this Convention (church) shall be a common purpose to do the will of God as Jesus revealed it and to co-operate in establishing the kingdom for which he lived and died.

> To that end we avow our faith in God as Eternal and All-Conquering Love, in the spiritual leadership of Jesus, in the supreme worth of every human personality, in the authority of truth known or to be known, and in the power of men of goodwill and sacrificial spirit to overcome all evil and progressively establish the kingdom of God.

To this was added the Liberty Clause and the 1803 and 1899 statements, with the notation that:

> These historic declarations of faith with liberty of interpretation are dear and acceptable to many Universalists. They are commended not as tests but as testimonies in the free quest for truth that accords with the genius of the Universalist Church. The conditions of fellowship in this Convention (church) shall be acceptance of the essential principles of the Universalist faith and an acknowledgement of the ecclesiastical jurisdiction of the Universalist General Convention.

The changes from the 1899 declaration are obvious: there is no mention of the Bible, Jesus is no longer referred to as Christ, the doctrine of universal salvation is included only obliquely through the affirmation of "God as Eternal and All-Conquering Love" and "the supreme worth of every human personality," and there is a strong emphasis on the Social Gospel, as evidenced by the statement twice calling for the establishment of the Kingdom of God, in part, at least, through human effort.

The Universalist and Unitarian denominations had strikingly similar experiences during the 1930s. Both were in an alarming state of decline, suffering financially from the depression and spiritually from a lost sense of purpose, and both were revived by the emergence of new leaders—Frederick May Eliot for the Unitarians, Robert Cummins for the Universalists.

Cummins, a vigorous forty-year-old who had served for a dozen years in the parish ministry, replaced Roger Etz as General Superintendent in 1938 and immediately went to work with a will. During his first year in office he traveled extensively, analyzing firsthand the state of the denomination. Almost everywhere he went, Cummins found evidence of disorganization, decline, and low morale, and in his first report to the General Convention in 1939 he shared his findings openly with the delegates. He pointed out that since 1910 the number of state conventions had decreased from forty-three to twenty-four, the number of churches from 819 to 544, the number of family units from 52,272 to 39,827. He called for "a renewed consciousness of worth, dignity, and confidence" to replace the despair and indifference he had found. It was time, he said, for Universalists to stop looking nostalgically at the past, to recapture their lost spirit of unity, and to rechannel their energies away from such uninspiring activities as "bean suppers and fourth-rate speakers."

To accomplish this, Cummins presented a "Forward Together" program based on four realistic objectives: a rigorous reevaluation and revision of the denomination's overall program; aggressive, unified field work; a restructuring of the denominational organization to eliminate confusion, inefficiency, and lack of focus; and a commitment of sufficient funds to support the other three objectives. Cummins also argued successfully for a change in name. The term "Universalist General Convention" was both confusing and inaccurate, he contended, implying only a meeting of delegates; the "Universalist Church of America" would more accurately

General Superintendent Robert Cummins and AUA President Frederick May Eliot, revitalizers of their respective denominations, meet in 1953.

describe the denomination as a whole. In 1942, after the necessary legalities had been attended to, the change became official.

By the end of his second year in office, Cummins was reporting "genuine progress on all fronts"; his watchword was "centralization," his goal "efficiency." Edna Bruner, one of a decreasing number of women ministers, was hard at work organizing the new Department of General Field Work, which had been created to combine the separate, overlapping efforts of the WNMA, GSSA, and YPCU (the women's, Sunday school, and youth organizations); Cummins himself was busily reorganizing the many headquarters activities into a number of departments with well-defined responsibilities. Given the historic Universalist distrust of centralized authority, opposition was inevitable; it surfaced strongly at the 1941 General Convention at Tufts (the first such meeting held on a college campus). Frank Adams of Illinois, a former president of the convention, spoke for many when he assailed the administration's "fatal policy of centralization," but Cummins defended himself both angrily and forcefully, and in the end a continuation of the "Forward Together" program was approved by a vote of the delegates.

Whatever their differences in organizational philosophy and leadership style, Universalists were stirred into action by their new superintendent. At the 1943 General Assembly (the name of the biennial meetings had been changed, too) Cummins reviewed with great satisfaction the progress made in the first five years of his leadership—church membership had increased significantly (it was actually constituency and not membership that had increased, constituency including all who are significantly related to a church, whether official members or not), the youth group had been revitalized, the deficit had been reduced, and the organizational changes had worked out well. Moreover, much of this had been accomplished during a time when the country was involved in a war that had diverted human resources and energy away from ecclesiastical concerns. Cummins, addressing that same General Assembly, also boldly affirmed his own convictions about the nature of the movement he was leading:

> Universalism cannot be limited either to Protestantism or to Christianity, not without denying its very name. Ours is a world fellowship, not just a Christian sect. For so long as Universalism *is* universalism and not partialism, the fel-

lowship bearing its name must succeed in making it un-
mistakably clear that *all* are welcome: theist and humanist,
unitarian and trinitarian, colored, and color-less. A circumscribed Universalism is unthinkable.

Cummins's call for a "colored and colorless" Universalism was
especially pertinent given the experience of Jeffrey Campbell, one
of the few African Americans ordained to the Universalist ministry
prior to this time. Campbell had graduated from the Theological
School at St. Lawrence in 1935 and had recieved his fellowship and
been ordained, but the State Superintendent had opposed both his
ordination and his earlier acceptance into seminary on the grounds
that it was a waste of denominational money to educate a "colored"
man. Later, after his sister had married a white seminarian,
Campbell carried on a verbal battle with the editor of the *Universalist Leader*, John van Schaick, after he had condemned the
marriage as "professionally irresponsible." Campbell's sister,
Marguerite Davis, would later serve on the UUA staff at 25 Beacon
Street.

Cummins's words, while they undoubtedly upset some of the
more conservative delegates, were warmly received by the younger
generation of ministers, and the following year's events seemed to
confirm the appropriateness of the direction in which Cummins
was pointing the denomination.

The Universalist Church of America (UCA) had been invited to
apply for membership in the Federal Council of the Churches of
Christ in America (the predecessor of the present National Council
of Churches) and in 1942 decided, after careful negotiations, to
accept the invitation. The Universalists' chief motivation, according to Cummins, was to join forces with other denominations in
addressing the pressing human needs resulting from the war; it
was felt, moreover, that the Washington Avowal, committing the
denomination "to cooperate in establishing the Kingdom for which
[Jesus] lived and died," provided sufficient theological grounds for
acceptance into such an explicitly Christian body. The executive
committee of the Federal Council of Churches, apparently divided
on the issue and stalling for time, failed to act on the application,
claiming that it was too brief and asking that it be resubmitted
with more content. Thus, in 1944 the Universalist trustees, acting
in accordance with a vote of the General Assembly, prepared and
submitted a new application for membership, only to have it

rejected by the Federal Council's executive committee by a vote of 12 to 6. Denominations voting for admission were the Congregational-Christian, Disciples of Christ, Quakers, Seventh Day Baptists, Colored Methodist Episcopal in America, and African Methodist Episcopal.

Voting against admission were the National Baptist Convention, Church of the Brethren, Evangelical and Reformed, Reformed Episcopal, Lutheran, Methodist, United Brethren, United Presbyterian, Presbyterian USA, and United Church of Canada. The Northern Baptist and Protestant Episcopal denominations also voted against admission, but specified that they would change their position if the Universalists would accept Jesus Christ as Divine Lord and Savior. Indeed, opposition to admission, led by the Presbyterians, was based squarely on theological grounds, because Universalists were regarded as not sufficiently Christocentric and too much like the Unitarians. G. Bromley Oxnam, the liberal Methodist bishop who was the council's president-elect, also opposed the application, fearing that admission of the Universalists would divide the council during his term in office.

For their part, the Universalist leadership, and Cummins in particular, felt they had been treated unfairly, discourteously, and in an unchristian manner. Two years later, after they had been persuaded to reapply only to be rejected again, the break with institutional Christianity was complete. As Angus MacLean of the St. Lawrence Theological School put it, "After being turned down twice as not being good Christians, we decided we should look somewhere else." Not all Universalists agreed with MacLean, however; they still saw their denomination as an integral, if unappreciated, part of Christendom. Thus, while the adage "We do not stand, we move" still held true, Universalists were not of one mind about the direction in which they should be moving.

Chapter Eight

"A Circumscribed Universalism Is Unthinkable"

A New Identity Emerging, 1945–1960

While the Christian wing of the Universalist Church of America, led by such dedicated ministers as Ellsworth Reamon of Syracuse, Seth Brooks of Washington, and Cornelius Greenway of Brooklyn, moved to strengthen the denomination's Christian witness, a new liberal wing of young ministers was emerging, encouraged by General Superintendent Robert Cummins, Clarence Skinner, Clinton Scott, and others. In between, less sure of their direction, moved much of the laity and many of the ministers. (The leadership of the UCA, like that of other denominations at this time, was dominated by men; it is possible that a similar division was occurring within the Association of Universalist Women—one suspects that its members were more interested in going on with the work of the church than in theological arguments, but that story needs to be researched and told!) The appearance on the scene of the new liberal wing, which espoused an "emergent Universalism" that would move beyond Christianity to universal religion, was prompted by a variety of factors, among them the impulse toward world community resulting from the Second World War, the perceived need for a new Universalist identity, and the double rejection of the UCA by the Federal Council of Churches.

Tracy Pullman, grandson of James Pullman and minister of the church in Detroit, summarized the liberals' vision in a 1946 sermon by calling for a new religion that is "greater than Christianity because it is an evolutionary religion, because it is universal rather than partial, because it is one with the spirit of science and is primarily interested in bringing out that which is God-like in man."

That same year, the *Universalist Leader* devoted a whole issue to a symposium on "One World Religion." Among the contributors were three young Massachusetts ministers, Albert Ziegler of Wakefield, John Wood of Attleboro, and Dana Klotzle of Wellesley Fells. Also contributing were Scott, who was about to assume the superintendency of the Massachusetts Universalist Convention, and Carleton Fisher of the newly organized Universalist Service Committee. While the emphases of the authors varied, a common thread ran through their articles—namely, the call to transform Universalism into a religion for one world, which, while honoring its Christian origins, nevertheless would welcome the truths of other religions on an equal basis. In short, the authors were calling for a "universalizing of Universalism." Emerson Hugh Lalone, who had just succeeded John van Schaick as editor of the *Leader*, while open to the writers' views, at the same time warned of the dangers of a shallow eclecticism, pointing out that "he who believes everything ends up believing nothing" and warning that "there is no easy route to world religious fellowship."

The need for a new Universalist identity was put forward forcefully the following year by Mason McGinness, minister in Lowell, in a sermon to the Massachusetts Convention:

> The truth is that, in many instances, the only thing that distinguishes the Universalist church from the neighboring Congregational, Baptist or Methodist church in some communities is the name, not the gospel that is preached, nor the program of education. . . . If the Universalist Church has no message, no program that is different from other churches in the community, nothing that is distinctive, then let's unite with some other church quickly. . . . We have been drifting and disintegrating.

That same year, Cummins, pushing his fellow Universalists toward a new identity, repeated in his report to the 1947 General Assembly his earlier conviction that "a circumscribed Universalism is unthinkable." Then, at the next biennial, Brainard Gibbons, the highly respected minister from Wausau, Wisconsin, in a sermon titled "New Wine and Old Skins," posed the basic question that many Universalists had been unwilling to address:

> Is Universalism a Christian denomination, or is it some-
> thing more, a truly universal religion? This issue is the
> most vital Universalism has ever faced, striking at the
> very base of its religious foundation, for Christianity and
> this larger Universalism are irreconcilable. A momentous
> decision must be made, and soon! Unless Universalism
> stands for something distinctive and affirmative, it falls in
> indistinguishable, negative nothingness—neither loved nor
> hated, just ignored!

Many in the Christian wing of the denomination were understandably upset by Gibbons's words, but this did not stand in the
way of his election to denominational leadership in the years that
followed—first as president in 1951, then as general superintendent two years later.

A major force for change came from a small group of recent
graduates of the Crane Theological School at Tufts known as the
Humiliati. (Their name, taken from that of an ancient Italian
order, means "the humble ones"; few thought the latter-day

Seven members of the Humiliati *with Massachusetts State Superintendent Clinton Lee Scott at Frederick Harrison's ordination in 1949.
(l-r): Earle MacKinney, Gordon McKeeman, David Cole, Scott, Harrison,
Albert Zeigler, Raymond Hopkins, and Keith Munson.*

Humiliati humble, though!) The group was originally formed so that its members could continue to enjoy the friendships, intellectual stimulation, and spiritual growth they had benefited from as seminarians and was modeled in large part after the Fraters of the Wayside Inn, a group of leading ministers who had met annually since 1903 in South Sudbury, Massachusetts, for worship, study, and fellowship. The *Humiliati* held yearly retreats from 1946 until 1954 in which they addressed issues in theology, worship, and liturgy. Committed to the renewal of their denomination via a universalized Universalism, they adopted the symbol of the off-center cross enclosed by a circle, which was later widely used in Universalist churches. The circle represented the all-embracing nature of Universalism; the off-center cross recognized Universalism's Christian roots while at the same time implying that Christianity was no longer necessarily central to the faith. When the symbol first appeared at the ordination of one of the *Humiliati*, Earle McKinney, it created a minor controversy; later, another member of the group, David Cole, stirred a second controversy by his insistence on being ordained to the Universalist ministry rather than to the Christian ministry.

The "emergent Universalism" espoused by the *Humiliati* was a theological blend, heavily influenced by the teachings of Bruce Brotherston and Clarence Skinner and at once "functional, naturalistic, theistic, and humanistic"; it was widely attacked for both its inconsistencies and its novelty. The group's liturgical and symbolic innovations, including the wearing of clerical collars, were also criticized as inconsistent with the Universalist tradition. In addition, many were upset by the *Humiliati's* political activities within the denomination; at the 1947 General Assembly they succeeded in having Mary Slaughter Scott, a "progressive," elected to the UCA Board of Trustees by first having her nominated from the floor and then encouraging "bullet balloting" in her behalf. Despite the many criticisms leveled against them, the group had many supporters and brought a much-needed infusion of creative energy into the denomination at a critical time in its history.

After the group disbanded, most of its members remained in close contact with each other, the majority in time becoming members of the Fraters of the Wayside Inn. Almost all went on to successful careers in the parish ministry, and most rose to positions of denominational leadership. Raymond Hopkins, for example, served on the Joint Merger Commission and later, after merger, as the first executive vice president of the Unitarian Universalist Association; Gordon McKeeman was elected to the UUA Board of Trustees for two terms, served as president of the Unitarian Universalist Service Committee, and later became president of the Starr King School for the Ministry; Charles Vickery held leadership positions in the Universalist and Unitarian Universalist Service Committees; Keith Munson chaired the Joint Interim Committee that recommended merger; Frederick Harrison went on to become superintendent of the Massachusetts and Connecticut state conventions; Leon Fay became director of the UUA Department of Ministry; Albert Ziegler and Earle McKinney both served as UUA district executives; and David Cole, after establishing a reputation as an effective social activist, served with distinction some of the UUA's largest congregations.

The concept of a "universalized Universalism" soon became institutionalized through the establishment of the experimental Charles Street Universalist Meeting House. In 1947 the Massachusetts State Convention had, on the urging of Skinner and Clinton Scott, its new superintendent, voted to establish a church in Boston, where there had been no Universalist church for years even though it was the site of denominational headquarters. The church would break new ground by offering a clear alternative to the city's Unitarian churches, which at that time were traditional and conservative. An historic church building in the heart of Boston was purchased, and Scott was instructed to recommend a minister. His choice was Kenneth L. Patton, at that time serving as minister of the First Unitarian Society of Madison, Wisconsin, a man known for his preaching and writing skills and his openness to innovation. The Massachusetts Convention's board of trustees accepted Scott's recommendation, and Patton was installed as minister of the Meeting House on February 2, 1949, in an impressive service attended by an overflowing crowd of Universalists from all over the state.

Almost at once, however, opposition arose to Patton's ministry. Patton was an outspoken naturalistic humanist, and his sermons and weekly radio broadcasts disturbed the more conservative, Christian-oriented Universalists in the area. In addition, many found him abrasive, tactless, and uncompromising. In time even Mary Scott, who, like her husband Clinton, had put a great deal of time and energy into establishing the new congregation, became

The interior of the Charles Street Meeting House in Boston was decorated with no less than 65 symbols from the world's religions.

exasperated with Patton. With opposition rising, the Massachusetts Convention refused to admit the Charles Street Meeting House into membership on the grounds that its program and preaching were not truly Universalist; however, the state convention did by a narrow vote agree to continue its financial support. Clinton Scott stoutly defended Patton on the grounds of freedom of the pulpit, congregational polity, and the noncreedal nature of Universalism, and in time the controversy subsided with the meeting house eventually accepted into Massachusetts Convention membership.

Meanwhile, Patton was at work creating new worship materials and reshaping the interior of the sanctuary to express the idea of a universal religion for one world. The pews were arranged "in the round," a large mural depicting the great nebula in Andromeda was mounted in the chancel, and religious symbols from all faiths and cultures were placed on the walls. The Charles Street Meeting House never attracted a large membership, partly because of its urban location, partly because of financial limitations, partly because of its experimental approach to worship, and perhaps partly because of Patton's personality. After he left in 1964, membership steadily declined, forcing the church to close its doors in the 1970s.

Although it never became the strong center of Universalism that Scott and its other founders had envisaged, the Charles Street Meeting House nevertheless made significant contributions to liberal religion. Chief among these were, first, the wealth of worship materials—responsive readings, meditations, opening and closing words, and hymn texts—written by Patton and distributed throughout both the Universalist and Unitarian denominations and later the UUA (many remain in use); and, second, the church's promotion of the idea of universal religion, a religion for one world, drawing on all sources of religious faith, knowledge, and practice.

Two significant developments growing out of the postwar desire for one united world were the ongoing support of the United Nations by Universalists and the formation of the Universalist Service Committee. The beginning of the Service Committee was a modest one. In October 1945, Carleton Fisher, who had resigned from his ministry in Buffalo to enter war-relief work, was commissioned to represent the Service Committee in Europe. In November he left for France, where he familiarized himself with the work of the Unitarian Service Committee, organized six years earlier. For the next two years Fisher worked as a joint representative of the two service committees, first in the Netherlands, distributing food and clothing, and then in Hungary, establishing a child-feeding program and distributing seed potatoes to farmers. Only after the Hungarian government forced him out of the country did he finally return to the United States. Six years later, Fisher, by then the director of an enlarged Universalist Service Committee, described it in the newsletter, *One Humanity,* as "a means, a way, a method, whereby we can demonstrate what we mean when we affirm the worth of every human personality, and the power of good will to create a better world."

From 1947 through the 1950s, much of the Service Committee's overseas work was devoted to the rehabilitation of postwar Germany, and in particular the care and relocation of displaced persons, especially youth who had been separated from their families and, in many cases, orphaned during the war. Gustav and Rebecca Ulrich, Charles Vickery, Helen MacKenzie, and Helen French, among others, gave leadership to this work. As part of the program, they set up summer work camps, and a number of Universalist youth came to Germany to volunteer their services. Work camps were also established in the United States, with volunteers operating educational and recreational centers, working in mental hospitals, and repairing church buildings. In time the Service Committee also took over support of the Jordan Neighborhood House in Virginia, the Ryder Community Center in Chicago, and the Nagano Center in Japan. In addition, it undertook numerous short-term projects to meet pressing human needs in the Middle and Far East. In 1953 Fisher, after serving as director for six years, resigned to return to the parish ministry; he was replaced by Dana Klotzle, who served in this capacity until merger with the Unitarian Service Committee in 1963. During its eighteen years of existence the Universalist Service Committee, with few financial resources but rich human resources, posted a remarkable record of achievement.

At the 1947 General Assembly, held on the St. Lawrence University campus, it had become apparent that forces were at work that could significantly reshape the future of the denomination. Ellsworth Reamon, completing his term as UCA president, had reported success in achieving the three major objectives of his presidency—a balanced budget, a better spirit within the denomination, and improved relations with the Unitarians. Fisher reported on his work with the Service Committee, inspiring support for an expanded program. The delegates, acting on the recommendation of a committee headed by Angus MacLean, voted to create a new denominational department of education. Superintendent Cummins renewed his plea for understanding Universalism as "a world fellowship, not a Christian sect". At this time the *Humiliati* first showed their strength as agents of change. Frederick May Eliot, president of the American Unitarian Association, shared his vision of a "United Liberal Church of America" that would include all religious liberals and urged the Universalists and the Unitarians to take the lead in creating it.

Despite the failure of the Free Church Fellowship during the administration of his predecessor, Louis Cornish, Eliot had persisted in his own efforts to form an inclusive body of religious liberals, this time making sure that there would be grassroots involvement in the process. Eliot's persistence paid off; the delegates heeded his words, and the following year a ten-member committee was appointed to meet with a similar committee from the AUA to explore the possibility of merger. The two committees found "no insuperable obstacles" and presented a joint resolution to the 1949 General Assembly recommending a process that, if followed to completion, would lead to a federal union based on "freedom of faith and congregational polity." After lengthy debate the delegates approved the resolution unanimously. Not wishing to see the mistakes of the previous decade repeated, Eliot and Cummins issued a joint statement clarifying the process. The first step, as they outlined it, was to poll the churches in both denominations about whether they even wanted to discuss the possibility of merger.

As it turned out, there was some real reluctance to do so, especially among the Universalists. As one of them put it, the Unitarians seemed more interested "in analyzing the nature of infinity than in the spirit of love. I feel that I ought to put on my company manners when I go into a Unitarian church."

Initially, it had been specified that at least 75 percent of the churches in each denomination would have to agree to the merger discussions, but when only 220 of the 304 certified Universalist churches, or 72 percent, voted in the affirmative, it was decided to lower the requirement to 60 percent, and the process went on. A temporary joint administrative board was then appointed to oversee combined services in religious education, public relations, and publications. In 1953 a more permanent arrangement was established when a joint assembly, meeting in Andover, Massachusetts, voted to establish the Council of Liberal Churches (Universalist-Unitarian), or CLC, to administer the three combined enterprises—the Universalists by a vote 257 to 12, the Unitarians unanimously. The Andover assembly, which was the first of four such joint biennial meetings held in conjunction with the Universalist General Assemblies, also authorized the creation of a twelve-member Joint Interim Committee. This committee was also charged with reporting to an assembly in 1955 on the details involved in effecting a merger, and on the feasibility of expanding combined services to include ministry and church extension.

A few months after the Andover assembly, Brainard Gibbons was installed as the new general superintendent of the UCA, succeeding Robert Cummins, who had served so wisely and well for fifteen years. During his tenure, Cummins had not only strengthened the organizational structure of the denomination but also had started it moving in a whole new direction. Gibbons held the position for only three years, but they were critical years during which he repeatedly challenged the denomination to provide his administration with the necessary authority and financial support to allow cooperation with the Unitarians to continue.

It soon became obvious to both denominations that financing the CLC in addition to their own operations was creating an almost unbearable burden. The CLC's Department of Public Information, with headquarters in New York City, was so underfinanced that its director, Roland Gammon, had to raise part of his own salary, and there were never sufficient funds to establish the joint publications program. When the Joint Interim Committee made its report to the 1955 joint biennial assembly, it surprised many in both denominations by going beyond the expected progress report on the operation of the CLC and recommending the formation of a Joint Merger Commission charged with preparing plans for the consolidation of the two denominations. The report, signed by all twelve members, asserted that "the Unitarians and Universalists hold enough in common to become one people"; moreover, the council arrangement was both too costly and too clumsy to work in the long term.

Many Universalists initially opposed the committee's proposal. Some were angered, feeling the committee had gone beyond its mandate; Ziegler feared that the democracy that Universalists cherished would be sacrificed in a merger; Reamon was convinced that the Universalists would simply be swallowed up and lose their identity; Gibbons saw the differences in polity and organization as too great to overcome. However, after prolonged debate the Universalist members of the committee persuaded the vast majority of their fellow Universalists to approve the proposal. Strong opposition to merger had also been voiced by A. Powell Davies, minister of All Souls' Church (Unitarian) in Washington and other Unitarians who regarded the Universalists as overly conservative. Nevertheless, the Unitarians also approved the proposal, and each denomination selected six members of the new commission.

The Universalists appointed Robert Wolley, later replaced by Raymond Hopkins; Carleton Fisher, later replaced by Robert McLaughlin; Max Kapp; Wilson Piper; Alan Sawyer; and Carl Westman. By fall of 1956 the commission's work was under way, with William Rice, minister of the Unitarian church in Wellesley Hills, Massachusetts, as its chair.

Just as the commission was beginning its work, Gibbons resigned as general superintendent, and Philip Giles, director of the UCA's Departments of Ministry and Church Extension, was chosen by the board of trustees to take his place. Giles, who had served as both a parish minister and an Air Corps chaplain, took office on January 23, 1957, his fortieth birthday. He gave the denomination energetic and effective leadership until consolidation in 1961. (The term "consolidation" was beginning to be used in place of "merger" to avoid the implication that one denomination was absorbing the other.) Giles immediately put in place a practical three-point program called Operation Bootstrap to formulate, study, and implement goals. The program emphasized the local church, with the denomination giving churches guidance with regard to process but carefully avoiding recommendations as to what the congregation's goals or programs should be. Giles and the board also initiated a four-year Universalist Advance program, with the goal of moving the denomination ahead "on all possible points."

The new superintendent was determined that whether or not it eventually merged with the Unitarians, the Universalist Church of America should be strengthened in every possible way. His efforts bore fruits. By the time Giles left office, many of the detailed recommendations made by a management consulting firm had been implemented; a number of congregations had erected new buildings, and others had renovated their existing facilities; a development program had been initiated to strengthen the denomination's financial base; the format and contents of both the *Universalist Leader* and the annual yearbook had been significantly improved; the Universalist Publishing House had been revitalized, and several basic books on Universalism had been produced; and communications within the denomination had been substantially strengthened.

In 1958, shortly after Giles took office, the Joint Merger Commission prepared a detailed 103-page manual titled "Merger and Alternatives" for distribution to the churches with an accompanying study guide. The manual presented a great deal of historical and organizational information, as well as up-to-date statistics about both denominations. The statistics made it clear that the consolidation, if it occurred, would be between two numerically unequal bodies. The American Unitarian Association reported 606 active societies (361 churches and 245 lay-led fellowships) with a total membership of 106,751; the Universalist Church of America reported 298 active societies (289 churches and nine fellowships) with a total membership of 42,858. Moreover, the AUA had experienced a dramatic gain in total membership since the end of the Second World War, while the UCA had undergone a small but significant decline. Predictably, then, some Unitarians feared that their remarkable growth might be slowed by the consolidation process.

The main body of the manual presented two basic plans for consideration, along with four alternatives, with all churches and fellowships urged to express their preferences through a plebiscite. The first plan called for complete merger (or consolidation) of the two denominations, and the second for an expanded Council of Liberal Churches; the four alternatives to these plans were maintenance of the *status quo*, withdrawal from cooperation, formation of an interdenominational council of liberal religious groups, or establishment of a committee on cooperation among liberal religious groups. In the plebiscite, approximately three-fourths of the churches voted for the first plan, and hence the commission prepared a detailed plan for consolidation, which was distributed just a month before the 1959 joint assembly. The plan, by and large, incorporated structures and procedures already in place in one or both of the denominations. Annual General Assemblies were called for, as was the establishment of regional organizations (later to become known as districts). State conventions could continue, but they would not be part of the basic organizational structure. An elected board of trustees would make policy decisions, guided by the actions of the General Assembly; an elected, unpaid moderator would preside at board meetings and General Assemblies; and an elected, salaried president would serve as chief executive officer. The plan reaffirmed congregational autonomy and the noncreedal basis for membership, and it proposed that the new denomination be named the Unitarian Universalist Association in recognition of the fact that both bodies were attached to their traditional names.

When the delegates assembled in Syracuse, New York, to consider the plan, feelings at times ran high. During a joint session that went on for five hours, nerves became frayed, and there were "frequent moments of great tension" and "intense differences of opinion." One heated debate involved the question of whether the purposes and principles in the proposed constitution should refer to "truths taught by Jesus" and "our Judeo-Christian heritage." Delegates voiced sharply conflicting opinions, and at one point the whole plan seemed in jeopardy, but they finally reached a compromise that omitted the reference to Jesus and changed the phrase "our Judeo-Christian heritage" to "*the* Judeo-Christian heritage."

Reamon, Cornelius Greenway, and Albert Perry of Cincinnati led the Universalist opposition, but in the end the plan was approved by a wide margin. The Universalist vote in favor was 238 to 33, the Unitarian vote 518 to 43, with three abstentions. Greenway left the meeting completely disgruntled, complaining about "steamroller tactics"; by contrast, Reamon took part in the Sunday morning service that marked the end of the historic assembly, offering a reading from Hebrews on the need for faith in the face of an uncertain future. As for Perry, he, too, accepted the decision and went on to a significant ministry of social action in Providence, Rhode Island. Paul Carnes, minister of the federated Unitarian-Universalist church in Buffalo, who later became president of the UUA, remarked that at the assembly "something happened to the Universalists. They met the Unitarians and found that Unitarians are, more or less, just like Universalists except that there are more of them and they make more noise." Two steps still remained before the process of consolidation would be complete: first another plebiscite of the churches, then final approval by delegate bodies of the two denominations meeting concurrently but separately.

Unitarians and Universalists had been talking about merger on and off for a century, but up until this point theological, sociological, and educational differences had kept them apart. Now those differ-

Dana McLean Greeley, president of the AUA, and Philip Randall Giles, general superintendent of the UCA, in 1959 before the vote for merger.

ences had been largely overcome; Unitarians had moved beyond their humanist-theist controversy of the 1920s and 1930s, Universalists had moved beyond their exclusively Christian orientation. In the process both bodies had become more willing to accept diversity within their ranks. To be sure, the ideal of a "universalized Universalism" for "one world" was still far from being realized; the Universalist Church of America was still a largely male-dominated, white, middle-class, American denomination with but tenuous ties to the rest of the world. The ideal, however, was there as an unavoidable challenge and as an important part of the theology of the *Humiliati* and many other ministers as they went out to serve congregations that were not always ready to accept it.

Despite significant opposition to the merger, when the plebiscite was held in early 1960, 79 percent of the Universalist and 91 percent of the Unitarian societies voted affirmatively.

(Incidentally, by then, under pressure from the Unitarians for accurate information, what was probably the most reliable census ever taken of Universalist membership had been completed. Russell Miller called the official total of 36,864 "the pitiful remnant of a church with such great promise," but this view seems unwarranted since, according to those denominational records which could in any way be considered reliable, the greatest number of members that had ever been claimed was 55,513 in 1917, and even this figure was probably inflated. Contrary to popular misconception, the Universalist denomination, based on official membership figures, had never been large.)

In May delegate bodies of the two denominations met in a special assembly in Boston to take the last step. Giles had emphasized that the plebiscite had really been little more than an opinion survey and that a large turnout of Universalists was needed for the special assembly. A record 430 delegates did, in fact, attend, and 365 of them voted to ratify the consolidation; the Unitarian vote was 725 to 143. Following the vote, a huge congregation gathered in Symphony Hall for a service of celebration; the pulpits from which Hosea Ballou had been ordained and William Ellery Channing had preached were appropriated for the occasion. Giles and Dana McLean Greeley, president of the AUA, together lit a large candle from two smaller ones to symbolize the union that was taking place. Frederick May Eliot had not lived to see his dream of merger realized, but Greeley, his successor, had been an equally strong supporter of the consolidation. After Donald

Harrington, John Haynes Holmes's successor at the Community
Church of New York, had proclaimed in his sermon the creation of
a new world faith, 2,000 Unitarian Universalists joined in a pledge
of allegiance to their new denomination:

> We, Unitarians and Universalists, children of the Judeo-
> Christian heritage, inheritors of the wisdom of the univer-
> sal prophets, eager to experience the insights of the great
> faiths of the world, open to all sources of inspiration,
> ancient and modern, determined to explore the boundless
> ocean of truth which lies about on every hand and on
> before, and welcoming into fellowship all men (sic) of
> whatever background of faith, here together on this night
> of Consolidation, conscious of the presence of the past, and
> of our urgent tasks, dedicate ourselves anew to the free and
> universal fellowship of all mankind that is the church to
> be.
>
> We declare our allegiance to the new Unitarian Universal-
> ist Association, and pledge our lives, our fortunes, and our
> faith to its high purpose and sure upbuilding.

While it would be another year before the final legalities were
completed, that night in May 1960 marked the true beginning of
the new denomination. As Russell Miller wrote in concluding his
two-volume history, "What the future would bring, no one could
really know. But the pledge of allegiance . . . stood as an affirmation
of the Larger Hope on the threshold of another era yet to unfold."

Chapter Nine

"A Bold, Fresh Enterprise of the Liberal Spirit"

Universalism's Contribution to the Merged Movement, 1961–1993

At the organizing meeting of the Unitarian Universalist Association, held in Boston in May 1961, a constitution and bylaws were adopted, and officers and trustees elected. Dana McLean Greeley, who had served as president of the American Unitarian Association since 1958, was elected as the UUA's first president over William Rice, chair of the Joint Commission on Merger, by a vote of 1,135 to 980 after a hotly contested campaign. Greeley had been the choice of the nominating committee, but many Universalists objected, thinking it inappropriate for either Greeley or Giles to be considered for the office; Rice, who, like Greeley, came from the Unitarian side of the merger, was then persuaded to accept nomination by petition. Among the Universalists elected to office were Anne Bowman as secretary, Carleton Fisher as vice president, and Earle McKinney, Carl Olson, Alan Sawyer, Carl Bays, Harmon Gehr, Nicholas Greene, and Clinton Scott as trustees. Marshall Dimock, who held membership in both Unitarian and Universalist churches, was chosen as moderator. Despite the criticism leveled at it over the choice of Greeley, the nominating committee had been careful to ensure that neither side would dominate the new Association's leadership. Later, Greeley's appointment of Raymond Hopkins as executive vice president helped reassure Universalists who had feared too strong a Unitarian influence. The Association's new president was installed in a service held at the Community

Church of New York in October 1961, with Max Kapp, Greeley's longtime friend, preaching the sermon. Unitarian Universalists, he said, were marching "into perilous and untried tomorrows . . . in a bold, fresh enterprise of the liberal spirit [and in] the splendid expectancy of a significant future." He offered no guarantees, however, only hope.

The newly adopted constitution and bylaws specified that all member churches and fellowships of the AUA and UCA had automatically become members of the UUA upon consolidation. In 1963 Cornelius Greenway's Universalist church in Brooklyn formally withdrew from membership but later, after Greenway's death, rejoined. Seth Brooks's National Memorial Church in Washington, while not withdrawing, distanced itself from other Unitarian Universalist churches in the area for many years in its advertisements; in time, however, it actively engaged itself in denominational affairs. A few other Universalist churches, mostly in the rural deep South, while technically members, have never participated in UUA affairs to any significant extent. However, the vast majority of churches and fellowships in both denominations accepted consolidation and the responsibilities that went with it. After 1961 a number of churches and fellowships expanded their names from "Universalist" or "Unitarian" to "Unitarian Universalist," and most new societies organized since consolidation have adopted names reflecting both traditions. The Silver Spring Universalist Church in suburban Washington, an outgrowth of National Memorial, was so enthusiastic about merger that it already had a sign with its new Unitarian Universalist name ready and waiting; as soon as its minister, David MacPherson, heard the news of consolidation, the sign went up!

The consolidation of the two denominations was quickly followed by the mergers of numerous Unitarian and Universalist organizations. The *Universalist Leader* and the *Unitarian Register* were quickly combined into the *Register-Leader*, predecessor to the present *World*. Each denomination had its Church of the Larger Fellowship, a "church by mail" designed to meet the needs of those without a church in their vicinity; the two merged in 1961, as did the two ministers' associations. Then in 1963 the service committees united, and that same year the Association of Universalist Women and the Unitarian Women's Alliance combined to form the Unitarian Universalist Women's Federation. The historical societies were the last pair to unite, in a 1978 merger that created the

Unitarian Universalist Historical Society. At the time of consolidation there were seventeen state conventions and one provincial convention in existence; three decades later only six were listed in the annual directory—those in New York, Pennsylvania, North Carolina, Georgia, Rhode Island, and Vermont/Quebec. The UUA regional districts had for the most part rendered the conventions obsolete as programmatic organizations; those that remained served principally as the distributors of income from invested funds. The Universalist Convention of North Carolina is an exception; it continues to sponsor retreats and workshops, mostly at its camp and conference center at Shelter Neck. In recent years it has welcomed new fellowships into its membership and, with its monthly newsletter, the *Tar Heel Universalist*, edited by Regina Burton of Red Hill, serves as a "cluster" organization for the Unitarian Universalist societies in the eastern part of the state. In addition to Shelter Neck, the camp and conference centers established by the Universalists at Ferry Beach in Maine, Unirondack in New York, and Murray Grove in New Jersey all continue to operate, as does the Clara Barton Camp for Diabetic Girls in Massachusetts.

A major disappointment to many from the Universalist side of the consolidation was the closing in the mid-1960s of the two existing Universalist seminaries, the Theological School at St. Lawrence and the Crane Theological School at Tufts. Still, some sort of change had been inevitable. Unitarian Universalists had begun to realize that four seminaries (St. Lawrence, Crane, Meadville/Lombard Theological School at Chicago, and Starr King School for the Ministry at Berkeley) were too many for one small denomination to support. In addition, the Harvard Divinity School, while not formally affiliated with the denomination, nevertheless had a strong Unitarian tradition and was continuing to prepare many students for the liberal ministry.

In anticipation of consolidation, the AUA Board of Trustees in 1959 had appointed a committee to study theological education, whose mission later was endorsed by the board of the UUA. The committee, chaired by Raymond Johnson, a former director of the AUA Department of Ministry, commissioned Harold Taylor, a distinguished educator and former president of Sarah Lawrence College, to make an independent study of the five seminaries and report his findings and recommendations. Published in 1962, Taylor's report, besides recommending numerous curriculum changes, also recommended that there be three centers for the education of Unitarian Universalist ministers—Meadville in the Midwest, Starr King in the West, and a new school in the East with a completely restructured program to be established on the Crane campus, using the combined resources of St. Lawrence and Crane. Taylor's report, which was highly critical of all the schools except Starr King, made a significant impact, at the same time creating a great deal of resentment and lowering student and faculty morale. The administration and trustees of the theological schools at St. Lawrence and Tufts did explore the creation of a new seminary at either Medford or New York City, and later there was some consideration of a 1964 General Assembly recommendation that both schools merge with either Meadville or Starr King. In the end, however, all negotiations failed, and the two schools were forced to close their doors.

The Theological School at St. Lawrence had been governed by its own board of trustees, separate from the rest of the university, and its financial resources have been preserved under the St. Lawrence Foundation for Theological Education, with the income providing scholarship support to seminarians preparing for the Unitarian Universalist ministry. After the school closed in 1965, its alumni association created awards in honor of the school's last two deans: the Angus H. MacLean Award for excellence in the field of religious education and the Max A. Kapp Award for the best student paper on the subject of Universalism. Over the 109 years of its existence St. Lawrence had successfully prepared many men and women for the ministry, but its isolated location made it increasingly hard to attract new students and to provide them with field work opportunities. During its last decade of operation, its faculty included such able scholars as Morton Scott Enslin in biblical studies; MacLean, Robert Cope, and Hugo Holleroth in religious education; Kapp and David Parke in church history; Kapp in homiletics; and Robert Tapp, Alfred Stiernotte, and Carl Hermann Voss in theology. Kapp, deeply saddened by the school's closing, accepted a position at UUA headquarters as Director of Interfaith and Overseas Relations; Holleroth joined the staff of the UUA Department of Education; the others either found new academic positions or accepted calls to the parish ministry.

Unlike the school at St. Lawrence, Crane was an integral part of Tufts; its program and policies were governed by the university's administration and trustees. During the fourteen-year tenure of

Benjamin B. Hersey, the school's last dean, the school was plagued by financial difficulties and operated largely with part-time faculty members with a high rate of turnover. Among those serving on the faculty during this period were Gene Reeves, Ernest Cassara, James Hunt, Robert L'H. Miller, Alan Seaburg, and Peter Baldwin. When Nils Wessell, the President of the university, who had been a strong Crane supporter, resigned in 1966, the school lost an important advocate. The erosion of university and denominational support and the increase of financial problems made the closing of Crane inevitable. The decision was made in June 1967; a year later, after the graduation of twelve students, the largest number since 1897, Crane, too, closed its doors. Like St. Lawrence, Crane had also successfully trained many men and women for the ministry during its ninety-nine years. Hersey, who, like Kapp, had been deeply saddened by the school's closing, accepted a call to the ministry of a small church in Essex, Massachusetts, dying there a few years later; many of the faculty members found academic positions elsewhere, and Reeves later served as dean at Meadville/Lombard for a number of years.

The loss of the two schools caused great bitterness among many from Universalist backgrounds. They felt that the process that had led to the closings had been overly hasty, initiated as it was by the Unitarians before consolidation; moreover, they felt that the so-called Barth Committee (named for its chair, Joseph Barth of King's Chapel), which had recommended to the General Assembly that the two schools turn over their resources to Meadville/Lombard and Starr King, had been "Unitarian dominated." In addition, many felt they were being "run over roughshod" at meetings by those from Unitarian backgrounds, whom they charged with insensitivity, especially for referring to Unitarian Universalists simply as "Unitarians." At one time this practice became so common even at meetings of the UUA Board of Trustees that fines were imposed on any trustee who succumbed to it. (Unfortunately, the practice survives, though perhaps less persistently than before, and rarely, if ever, at UUA board meetings!) And the joking suggestion that a shorter name for the denomination be adopted by taking the first two syllables of "Universalist" and combining them with the last three syllables of "Unitarian" was not always considered funny. Those from the Unitarian side of consolidation sometimes accused those from the Universalist side of paranoia; they in turn were themselves accused of arrogance, elitism, and a failure to appreciate the Universalist tradition. At the same time many people from both traditions embraced consolidation with enthusiasm, others at least accepted it with equanimity, and still others barely noticed it. With the passage of time much of the uneasiness over consolidation disappeared. For one thing, many from the Unitarian side of the merger were slowly beginning to appreciate the richness of the Universalist tradition. In addition, the presence in leadership positions of men and women who had come from the Universalist side not only helped others from their side see that they were not being neglected, but also showed those from the Unitarian side that consolidation had brought with it a source of strong new leadership. Anne Bowman, who had been elected secretary of the new association, had done such an excellent job that in 1965 she won the denomination's highest honor, its Award for Distinguished Service to the Cause of Unitarian Universalism; people like Scott, Gehr, and McKeeman had served, or were to serve, on the Board of Trustees; Giles, Hopkins, and Kapp held important positions on the headquarters staff; so, too, did Dorothy Spoerl, Alice Harrison, Edna Bruner, George Spencer, and Carl Seaburg; Russell Lockwood, William DeWolfe, Ziegler, McKinney, and others were or would be serving as district executives; Dorothy Chapman and Drusilla Cummins would become presidents of the Women's Federation; and many others also could be named. In time, anyone with eyes to see and ears to hear could tell that the Universalist branch of the new UU family had brought with it not only a rich heritage from the past but also strength for the present and future. (Later, Donald Thompson, Scott, Spoerl, Kenneth Patton, Cummins, and John Cummins, the son of the former general superintendent, would win the Award for Distinguished Service to the Cause of Unitarian Universalism, just as Bowman had done earlier.)

In 1970 Unitarian Universalists celebrated the 200th anniversary of John Murray's meeting with Thomas Potter on the Jersey coast and the preaching of his first sermon in America. They observed the occasion with special programs at Murray Grove, Gloucester, and the General Assembly, as well as in numerous local churches. The denomination was at a low point of morale then, having just gone through divisive controversies over black empowerment and the war in Southeast Asia, so most of the celebrations were low-key. One very positive result of the observance was the publication of *American Universalism: A Bicenten-*

nial Essay by George Huntston Williams of the Harvard Divinity
School. Williams, who comes from a strong Unitarian background,
had been commissioned by the Universalist Historical Society to
deliver a one-hour lecture, but he quickly became so engrossed in
his work that he produced an 89-page monograph, which has
become something of a classic. One of the essay's major contributions was to present "a fresh typology of Universalist positions,
shown in their 1870 expressions as well as in their origins and
recent development." As James Hunt writes in the preface, "No
scholar has delved so deeply into the whole range of Universalist
theology since Richard Eddy, eighty-five years ago, and from this
close examination of dozens of books and tracts, Dr. Williams has
given us a wholly new set of categories for comprehending the
dialectics of change in the theology of Universalism."

Williams, after acknowledging that by the time of the Gloucester
centennial in 1870 "the peculiarly Christocentric humanitarian
'Calvinistic' Universalism of John Murray" had been "transcended
and transmuted in . . . new theories of salvation," then identifies
three conceptions of Universalism that were current at that time:
first, "Christian Universalism," which he subdivides into
"Origenistic-Arminian-Unitarian Universalism," as expounded at
the centennial by A. A. Miner, and "Universalism: A Christian Sect
or Branch of the Church of Christ," as expounded by Richmond
Fisk, William Ryder, Elbridge Gerry Brooks, and Edwin Chapin;
second, "Universalism: the American Church of the Future and the
Civilized World," as explicated by Israel Washburn and Mary
Livermore; and third, "Universalism: the World Religion of the
Graeco-Roman World and the Emergent World Civilization," as
exemplified in the writings of Herman Bisbee and Adin Ballou,
neither of whom attended the centennial. Williams then traces the
evolution of these views into the liberal "Universal Christianity" of
the 1890s, which in turn evolved into the "Universal Religion" of
Clarence Skinner, Robert Cummins, Kenneth Patton, and the
Humiliati. Williams ends his essay with the following conclusion:

> American Universalism is a much more complex move-
> ment than American Unitarianism. The devolution of the
> doctrine of the Trinity with attendant philanthropic and
> eventually sociocritical concerns is much easier to follow in
> the surviving documentation and to rehearse in a standard
> denominational history than the universalization of Chris-

tianity with attendant philanthropic concerns *intercon-nected* at one and the same time and often in the same person (a) with America the redeemer nation of manifest global destiny, (b) with the socio-political model of the ancient Church nurtured in, but critical of, the Roman imperial *oikoumene,* and (c) with the restoration of that primitive ideal both in organized religion and in society at large in an orientation that has been at times not only futurist but eschatologically millenialist. . . .

By the mid-twentieth century there were only three de-nominational alternatives left [for Universalists]: repristination as one more Protestant denomination re-gathered in the fold with others in the Council of Churches, nationalist democratic faith, or the global humanism of world religion. The first option was indeed tried, unsuc-cessfully, in the 1940s. Despite the Americanist motif from Winchester through Washburn, the denomination had too much experience of being outside the mainstream to be willing to acquiesce in any uncritical Christian national-ism. Thus in the end it chose after nearly two centuries to merge with the very denomination whose name signaled the very doctrine by which Murray's christocentric Uni-versalism had been undone from within and from without. . . .

On the two hundredth anniversary of the landing of the humane and all-embracing John Murray at Good Luck on the Atlantic coast we can with him and in the encouraging company of generations of valiant and extraordinarily happy and motivated people, called Universalists, count on more than "good luck" for the century ahead, not wholly because of the inherent and unambiguous goodness of men [sic]— on this we have been sobered and perhaps even alarmed— but because of the sustaining powers in the cosmos, which, as Universalists so early perceived, is at once our celestial and earthly home.

The 1970 bicentennial observances and, in particular, Williams's essay significantly increased the appreciation of the Universalist contribution to the merged movement. Nine years later, the first volume of Russell Miller's monumental history of Universalism, *The Larger Hope*, appeared, and in 1985, the second volume. This detailed study, also commissioned by the Universalist Historical Society and dealing principally with the period from 1770 to 1961, has been the basic source for numerous articles, term papers, and lectures, as well as for this short history. Inspired in part, at least, by the writings of Williams and Miller, more and more scholars are beginning to work in the field of Universalist history, as shown by the steady increase in publications, lectures, seminars, and workshops on the subject. To give but two examples, the John Murray Distinguished Lectureship program, established in 1987 by the Murray Grove Association to "educate, remind and celebrate the contribution of Universalism to the Unitarian Universalist movement," has sponsored annual lectures at the General Assembly, and the New York State Convention of Universalists has included an address on Universalist theology as part of its annual meetings ever since 1975. An exciting historical discovery was made in the early 1980s by Gordon Gibson, at that time serving congregations in Mississippi; he located the Judith Sargent Murray papers, long thought to have been destroyed, in the attic of an antebellum mansion in Natchez. The papers, which included copies of letters Judith sent to her husband over many years, shed a great deal of light on their relationship and on John Murray's ministry. Through Gibson's persistent efforts, the papers have been preserved and microfilmed by the Mississippi State Department of Archives and History. Out of all this ongoing effort, the richness of the Universalism heritage has begun to come alive to contemporary Unitarian Universalists.

In 1985 the Unitarian Universalist Association passed another milestone. After a careful process that lasted several years, the UUA adopted a new set of principles to replace those adopted at Syracuse in 1959 and later revised several times. The new principles read as follows:

We, the member congregations of the Unitarian Universalist Association, covenant to affirm and promote:

- The inherent worth and dignity of every person;
- Justice, equity and compassion in human relations;
- Acceptance of one another and encouragement to spiritual growth in our congregations;

- A free and responsible search for truth and meaning;
- The right of conscience and the use of the democratic process within our congregations and in society at large;
- The goal of world community with peace, liberty and justice for all;
- Respect for the interdependent web of all existence of which we are a part.

The living tradition we share draws from many sources:

- Direct experience of that transcending mystery and wonder, affirmed in all cultures, which moves us to a renewal of the spirit and an openness to the forces which create and uphold life;
- Words and deeds of prophetic women and men which challenge us to confront powers and structures of evil with justice, compassion and the transforming power of love;
- Wisdom from the world's religions which inspires us in our ethical and spiritual life;
- Jewish and Christian teachings which call us to respond to God's love by loving our neighbors as ourselves;
- Humanist teachings which counsel us to heed the guidance of reason and the results of science, and warn us against idolatries of the mind and spirit.

(Note: The addition to this statement of a sixth source, that of earth-centered traditions, received preliminary approval at the 1992 General Assembly; final passage is anticipated in 1993.)

Grateful for the the religious pluralism that enriches and ennobles our faith, we are inspired to deepen our understanding and expand our vision. As free congregations we enter into this covenant, promising to one another our mutual trust and support.

Except for the seventh principle, which has at least its major roots in the environmental concerns of the postmerger period, the principles are grounded in varying degrees in both the Universalist and Unitarian traditions. The first principle, however, affirming the inherent worth and dignity of every person, is predominantly Universalist in character, rooted historically in the conviction that *all* are worthy of salvation; similarly, the fourth principle, affirming the need for a free and responsible search for truth and meaning, has a predominantly Unitarian ring to it, reflecting the traditional Unitarian stress on learning and intellect. And while the goal of world community identified in the sixth principle certainly is strongly rooted in the Unitarian tradition, it clearly comes out of the global humanism and "one world" religion emphasized in much of twentieth-century Universalist theology.

Likewise, the five sources of the living Unitarian Universalist tradition can be found in both branches of the merged movement, though not always with equal emphasis. "The transforming power of love" and the response "to God's love by loving our neighbors as ourselves," while certainly themes to be found in Unitarianism, have been even more central to Universalism; on the other hand, reliance on humanist teachings has been more central to Unitarianism. All this is to the good. The merger, commonly considered one of "heart and head" or of "love and intellect," has given the merged movements a strength and wholeness that neither movement had had by itself.

Some years ago, the author identified seven values that Universalists brought with them to the merger: a theology founded on the affirmation of love; a thoroughly democratic church government; a social conscience motivated by their belief in the supreme worth of every human person; a conviction that liberal religion can and should speak to all sorts and conditions of people; an insistence on the equality of women and men in both church and society; a recognition that liberal religion requires emotional warmth as well as intellectual rigor; and, finally, the great vision of inclusiveness implied by the Universalist name. In retrospect he realizes that on the question of the equality of women and men, male Universalists were not nearly as insistent as their faith required, but with that qualification, the list still appears to him as essentially valid, and those seven values continue to inform and challenge contemporary Unitarian Universalism.

Of all these values, the last—that of the great vision of inclusiveness—presents the greatest challenge. "Universalism" remains "the biggest word in the English language," waiting to find much fuller expression in the life of the Unitarian Universalist Association. The admission into membership of the Unitarian Universalist Church of the Philippines; the "Sister Church" program linking American and Transylvanian churches; the attempts to organize societies in parts of the former Soviet Union; the strengthening of ties with liberal religious congregations and movements around the world, both directly and through the International Association for Religious Freedom; the organization of churches specifically designed to attract and serve the needs of African Americans; the initiation of programs to promote the full participation of people without regard to race, color, national origin, ethnic background, age, gender, affectional or sexual orientation, disability, or socioeconomic status—all these have been undertaken during the presidencies of Eugene Pickett and William Schulz in an attempt to make the denomination more truly "Universalist." Significant progress has been realized, particularly with respect to the inclusion of women, African Americans, gays, and lesbians in leadership positions. A great deal more remains to be accomplished, however, for despite these efforts, the membership is still largely white, middle-class, and American. The vision, though, endures; the challenge is ongoing.

In the 200 years since that group of people who called themselves Universalists gathered in General Convention in the village of Oxford, Massachusetts, for a day of preaching, prayer, fellowship, mutual support, and organizational business, the denomination they were unknowingly creating has evolved in ways that would have amazed and perhaps disturbed them. Nevertheless, the strong thread of history runs uninterrupted through those 200 years, binding them and present-day Unitarian Universalists firmly together in the shared affirmation of a Love that transcends both time and place.

References

Almost all of the subjects covered in this book are based at least in part on material found in Russell E. Miller's two-volume history of American Universalism, *The Larger Hope* (Boston: Unitarian Universalist Association, 1979, 1985). In addition, subjects dealing with the period through 1886 are in most cases based in part on Richard Eddy's two-volume history, *Universalism in America* (Boston: Universalist Publishing House, 1884, 1886). In cases where reference is made to the *Proceedings of the Unitarian Universalist Historical Society*, the citation will be to *PUUHS*.

Chapter One

Major sources: Miller, Vol. I, Chapters 1, 2, 3, and 5; and Eddy, Vol. I, Chapters II, III, IV, and V. Other sources: John Murray, *The Life of Rev. John Murray* (Boston: Marsh, Capen and Lyon, 1833); Janet H. Bowering, "Compelling Landfall," The 1992 John Murray Distinguished Lecture; Albert D. Bell, *The Life and Times of Dr. George de Benneville (1703–1793)* (Boston: Universalist Church of America, 1953); Clinton Lee Scott, *The Universalist Church of America: A Short History* (Boston: Universalist Historical Society, 1957), chapters I and II; Gordon D. Gibson, "The Rediscovery of Judith Sargent Murray," in *"Not Hell, But Hope,"* ed. Charles A. Howe (Murray Grove Association, 1991), pp. 69–90; Howe, "How Human an Enterprise: The First Universal Society in Boston During John Murray's Ministry," *PUUHS*, Vol. XXII, Part I (1990–1991), pp. 19–34; Howe, "British Universalism: Elhanan Winchester, William Vidler and the Gospel of Universal Restoration," *Transactions of the Unitarian Historical Society*, Vol. XVII, No. 1 (September 1979), pp. 1–14; Archives, Massachusetts Historical Society, *Record Book*, Independent Christian Society, Gloucester, Tax List, 1794. Sources of major quotations: Ernest Cassara, "The New World of John Murray," in *"Not Hell, But Hope,"* pp. 16–17, for the quote from Abigail Adams; Henry Cheetham, *Unitarianism and Universalism* (Boston: Beacon Press, 1962), p. 80, for the charge by John Murray to his fellow ministers; Archives, Massachusetts Historical Society, letter to "My dear Friend," December 19, 1789, for Murray's opinion of Winchester; letter to a Philadelphia friend, Eddy, Vol. 1, pp. 337–338, for Murray's report on Connecticut; Eddy, Vol. 1, pp. 359–379, for quotes from Murray's *Some Hints Relative to the Forming of a Christian Church;* Archives, Massachusetts Historical Society, *Record Book*, First Universal Society in Boston, for quotes concerning Murray's call and installation.

Chapter Two

Major sources: Miller, Vol. I, Chapters 2, 3, 5, and 6; Eddy, Vol. I, Chapters VI and VII; Eddy, Vol. II, Chapters I, II, and III; and Cassara, *Hosea Ballou: The Challenge to Orthodoxy* (Boston: Beacon Press and Universalist Historical Society, 1961). Other sources: Howe, "Under Orders from No Man: Universalist Women Preachers Before the Civil War," in *"Not Hell, But Hope,"* pp. 32–35; Hosea Ballou, *A Treatise on Atonement* (15th ed.; Boston: Universalist Publishing House, 1959); Howe, "How Human an Enterprise"; A. A. Miner, "The Century of Universalism," in *The Memorial History of Boston* (Boston: 1881), Vol. 3. Sources of major quotations: Archives, Massachusetts Historical Society, *Record Book*, First Universal Society in Boston, for quote regarding Winchester replacing Murray as delegate; Eddy, Vol. II, pp. 432–433, for quote from Circular Letter, 1794 convention; Nathaniel Stacy, *Memoirs of the Life of Nathaniel Stacy* (Columbus, Pa, 1850), for quotes from Stacy.

Chapter Three

Major sources: Miller, Vol. I, Chapters 6, 8, 10, 13, 15, 18, 19, 20, 21, and 23; Eddy, Vol. II, Chapter IV; and Cassara, *Hosea Ballou*. Sources of major quotations: Cassara, *Hosea Ballou*, p. 121, for quote from Wood and p. 167 for quote from Parker; Miller, Vol. II, p. 287, for quote from Miller about periodicals.

Chapter Four

Major source: Miller, Vol. I, Chapters 1, 8, 17, 18, 19, 21, and 22. Other sources: Cassara, *Universalism in America: A Documentary History* (2nd ed.; Boston: Skinner House, 1984), pp. 209–211; Conrad Wright, "A History of the Practice of Congregational Polity in Unitarian and Universalist Churches," work in progress; Howe, "Daniel and Mary Livermore: The Biography of a Marriage," *PUUHS*, Vol. XIX, Part II (1982–1983), pp. 14–35; Gibson, "The Rediscovery of Judith Sargent Murray," in *"Not Hell, But Hope,"* p. 77; A. H. Saxon, *P.T. Barnum: The Legend and the Man* (New York: Columbia University Press, 1989), p. 63. Sources of major quotations: Eddy, Vol. II, pp. 479–482 for quote from Eddy; Oscar Sherwin, *Prophet of Liberty: The Life and Times of Wendell Phillips* (New York: Bookman Associates, 1958), p. 236 for quote from Garrison; Miller, Vol. I, p. 630 for Miller's quote on the abolitionist movement; Howe, "Under Orders from No Man," in *"Not Hell, But Hope,"* pp. 37–46, for Whittemore quotes; George Huntston Williams, *American Universalism: A Bicentennial Historical Essay* (2nd ed.; Boston: Skinner House, 1976), p. 59 for quote from Rush.

Chapter Five

Major source: Miller, Vol. I, Chapter 29; Miller, Vol. II, Chapters 1, 2, 6, 12, 13, 21, 22, 23, 24, and 25. Other sources: Wright, *Congregational Polity*; Howe, "An Uneasy Alliance: Unitarians and Universalists During the Bellows Years (1839–1882)," *PUUHS*, Vol. XXI, Part I (1987–1988), pp. 33–42; Howe, "Daniel and Mary Livermore," *PUUHS*, Vol. XIX, Part II (1982–1983), pp. 14–35; David Johnson, "Augusta Chapin: Universalist Pioneer, Missionary, Prophet," in *"Not Hell, But Hope,"* pp. 53–67; Charlotte Coté, *Olympia Brown: The Battle for Equality* (Racine, Wis.: Mother Courage Press, 1988); Catherine F. Hitchings, *Universalist and Unitarian Women Ministers*, published as Volume X of the *Journal of the Universalist Historical Society*, 1975.

Chapter Six

Major source: Miller, Vol. II, Chapters 3, 6, 9, 18, 19, 20, 23, 24, 25, 26, and 27. Other sources: Eddy, Vol. II, p. 419; Elmo Robinson, *American Universalism* (Jericho, NY: Exposition Press, 1970), p. 161. Sources of major quotations: Miller, Vol. II, p. 458, for quote from Miller on Japan mission, p. 350, for quote from Miller on Shinn, and pp. 733–735, for "A Declaration of Social Principles"; Johnson, *Chicago Universalism* (Brookline, Mass.: Philomath Press, 1991), p. 149, for the first Chapin quote; Johnson, "Augusta Chapin," p. 67, for the second Chapin and the Brown quotes; Williams, *American Universalism*, p. 55, for quotes from Eaton and Powers.

Chapter Seven

Major source: Miller, Vol. II, Chapters 5, 21, 25, 26, 29, 30, 31, and 32. Other sources: UUA Commission on Appraisal, *Empowerment: One Denomination's Quest for Racial Justice, 1967–1982* (Boston: Unitarian Universalist Association, 1983), pp. 16, 20; Mrs. L. M. Hammond, *History of Madison County, State of New York* (Syracuse, N.Y.: Truair, Smith & Co., 1872). Sources of major quotations: Hitchings, *UU Women Ministers*, p. 6 for quote from Etz; Williams, *American Universalism*, p. 82, for quotes from Cummins and Williams; Cassara, *Universalism in America*, p. 253, for quote from Fisher; Miller, Vol. II, pp. 570–571, for quote from Eliot, pp. 579–580, for quote from Miller regarding fear of loss of identity, and p. 602, for quote from Miller on failure of the Free Church Fellowship; quote from MacLean, ca. 1960, is from author's memory.

Chapter Eight

Major source: Miller, Vol. II, Chapters 27, 32, and 33. Other sources: Howe, "Clinton Lee Scott, Revitalizer of Universalism," *PUUHS*, Vol. XXI, Part II (1989), pp. 12–18, for material on Patton and the Charles Street

Meeting House; Kenneth L. Patton, *A Religion for One World* (Boston: Beacon Press and Meeting House Press, 1964), for information on the Meeting House; *Christian Leader*, Vol. CXXIX (September 20, 1947), pp. 411–424, for material on the 1947 General Assembly; issues of the *Universalist Leader*, 1957–1961, were searched for information on Giles and his accomplishments; "An Informational Manual" and "A Discussion Guide," both prepared by the Joint Commission on Merger (Wellesley Hills, Mass. 1958), for statistical information and details of proposed plans and alternatives; and Universalist directories and yearbooks, 1864–1959, for statistical information. The figure for total Universalist membership at the time of consolidation is from Miller, Vol. II, p. 29. Sources of major quotations: Williams, *American Universalism*, p. 84, for the quote from Pullman; Miller, Vol. II, p. 634, for the McGinness and Gibbons quotes, and p. 665, for the pledge of allegiance; Emerson Hugh Lalone, *And Thy Neighbor as Thyself* (Boston: Universalist Publishing House, 1959), p. 104, for the Fisher quote.

Chapter Nine

Major sources: Miller, Vol. II, Chapters 16, 17, and 33; and *A Comprehensive Plan of Education for the Unitarian Universalist Ministry* (Boston: Unitarian Universalist Association, 1962). Other sources: UUA directories; Williams, *American Universalism*; Gibson, "The Rediscovery of Judith Sargent Murray," in *"Not Hell, But Hope,"* pp. 69–74; *The Universalist Heritage: The Relevance of Universalism—Past, Present and Future* (New York State Convention of Universalists, 1990); Howe, "Why I Am a Universalist," *Hoosier Voice of Fellowship*, Vol. 37, No. 2 (January 27, 1982), pp. 1–2. Sources of major quotations: James D. Hunt in Williams, *op. cit.*, p. iii, for quote from preface; Williams, *op. cit.*, pp. 86–89 for quote from conclusion.

Sources of Quotations in Chapter Titles

1. "Not Hell, But Hope"—John Murray, charge to his fellow ministers, quoted in Henry Cheetham, *Unitarianism and Universalism* (Boston: Beacon Press, 1962), p. 80.

2. "The Doctrine of Atonement Made Rational"—Section Heading No. 110 in Hosea Ballou, *A Treatise on Atonement* (15th ed.; Boston: Universalist Publishing House, 1959), p. 106.

3. "The Prominent Heresy of Our Times"—Title of Chapter 8, Russell Miller, *The Larger Hope: The First Century of the Universalist Church in America, 1770–1870* (Boston: Unitarian Universalist Association, 1979), p. 159.

4. "To Begin a Better State of Things"—Hosea Ballou 2nd, Occasional Sermon, 1847 Universalist General Convention, quoted in Ernest Cassara, *Universalism in America: A Documentary History of a Liberal Faith* (2nd ed.; Boston: Unitarian Universalist Association, 1984), p. 211.

5. "No Doctrine Not Clearly Taught in the Bible"—from an essay in the *Universalist Leader* published in 1873, quoted in Miller, *The Larger Hope: The Second Century of the Universalist Church in the United States, 1870–1970* (Boston: Unitarian Universalist Association, 1985), p. 77.

6. "Improve the Property or Move Off the Premises"—James M. Pullman, an address to the 1895 American Congress of Liberal Religious Societies, quoted in Miller, Vol. II, 1985, pp. 144–145.

7. "We Do Not Stand, We Move"—Lewis B. Fisher, *Which Way? A Study of Universalists and Universalism* (Boston: 1921), quoted in Cassara, *op. cit.,* p. 253.

8. "A Circumscribed Universalism Is Unthinkable"—Robert Cummins, address to the General Convention in 1943, quoted in George Huntston Williams, *American Universalism* (2nd ed., revised; Boston: Skinner House, 1976), p. 82.

9. "A Bold, Fresh Enterprise of the Liberal Spirit"—Max Kapp, sermon at the installation of Dana McLean Greeley as first president of the Unitarian Universalist Association, 1961, quoted in Miller, Vol. II, 1985, p. 665.

Appendix

**Presidents of the Universalist General Convention and
the Universalist Church of America**

1957–1961	Rev. Carleton Fisher
1953–1957	Alan F. Sawyer
1951–1953	Rev. Brainard Gibbons
1947–1951	Harold S. Latham
1943–1947	Rev. Ellsworth C. Reamon
1939–1943	Louis Annin Ames
1935–1939	Rev. W. H. MacPherson
1931–1935	Victor A. Friend
1927–1931	Rev. Frank D. Adams
1923–1927	Rev. John Murray Atwood
1919–1923	Roger Sherman Galer
1915–1919	Rev. Lee McCollester
1911–1915	Rev. Marion D. Shutter
1907–1911	Hon. Charles L. Hutchinson
1903–1907	Hon. Frank P. Bennett
1895–1903	Hon. Charles L. Hutchinson
1891–1895	Hon. Henry B. Metcalf
1887–1891	Hon. Hosea W. Parker
1885–1887	Rev. Edwin C. Sweetser
1877–1885	John D. W. Joy
1875–1876	Rev. Henry W. Rugg
1874–1875	Hon. Sidney Perham
1873–1874	Gen. Olney Arnold
1872–1873	Rev. A. A. Miner
1871–1872	Hon. Moses Humphrey
1870–1871	Rev. W. H. Ryder
1869–1870	Hon. Sidney Perham
1867–1869	Rev. J. G. Bartholomew
1866–1866	H. D. Williams, Esq.
1865–1866	E. G. Hall, Esq.

1864–1865   John T. Gilman, Esq.

Source: Copies of the *Universalist Record* and the *Year Book*.
No presidents listed prior to 1864; only standing clerks.

Presidents of the Association of Universalist Women and Its Predecessor Organizations

1961–1963	Edna Whippen
1957–1961	Helen Hamlin
1953–1957	Laura S. Hersey
1949–1953	Marjorie L. Springall
1945–1949	Jeannette C. Mulford
1941–1945	Corinne H. Brooks
1937–1941	Madelyn H. Wood
1933–1937	Alice T. Walker
1929–1933	Hazel I. Kirk
1925–1929	Grace Vallentyne
1921–1925	Ethel M. Allen
1917–1921	Marietta B. Wilkins
1913–1917	Minnie J. Ayres
1909–1913	Theresa A. Williams
1905–1909	Emma F. Foster
1903–1905	Zelia E. Harris
1902–1903	Florence K. Crooker
1891–1902	Cordelia A. Quinby
1880–1891	M. Louise Thomas
1869–1880	Caroline A. Soule

Source: Miller, Vol. II; copies of the AUW *Year Book*

General Superintendents of the General Convention and the UCA

1957–1961	Rev. Philip R. Giles
1953–1956	Rev. Brainard Gibbons
1938–1953	Rev. Robert Cummins
1928–1938	Rev. Roger Etz
1917–1928	Rev. John Smith Lowe
1907–1916	Rev. William H. McGlauflin
1898–1907	Rev. Isaac M. Atwood

Source: Miller, Vol. II.

Selected Bibliography

Basic Reading

Miller, Russell E. *The Larger Hope: The First Century of the Universalist Church in America, 1770–1870.* Boston: Unitarian Universalist Association, 1979.

_____. *The Larger Hope: The Second Century of the Universalist Church in America, 1870–1970.* Boston: Unitarian Universalist Association, 1985.

General Reading

Universalism in America: A Documentary History of a Liberal Faith. Edited by Ernest Cassara. 2nd ed. Boston: Skinner House, 1984.

Williams, George Huntston. *American Universalism: A Bicentennial Historical Essay.* 2nd ed. Boston: Skinner House, 1976.

Contemporary Newspapers, Magazines, and Journals

Proceedings of the Unitarian Universalist Historical Society (PUUHS)

Tar Heel Universalist

Unitarian Universalism: Selected Essays

Unitarian Universalist Christian

Universalist Herald

World: The Journal of the Unitarian Universalist Association

Denominational History

(supplementing the listings in Miller, Volumes I and II)

Ballou, Hosea. *A Treatise on Atonement.* Introduction by Ernest Cassara. 16th ed. Boston: Skinner House, 1986.

Bowering, Janet. "Compelling Landfall" (The 1992 John Murray Distinguished Lecture).

Bressler, Ann Lee. "Popular Religious Liberalism in America, 1770-1880: An Interpretation of the Universalist Movement." PhD Dissertation. Charlottesville, VA: University of Virginia, 1992.

Broadway, J. William. "Universalist Participation in the Spiritualist Movement of the Nineteenth Century," *PUUHS*, Vol. XIX, Part I (1980–1981).

Buck-Glenn, Judith. "Universalism Alive!" *Unitarian Universalist Christian*, Vol. 46, Nos. 3–4 (Fall/Winter, 1991).

Cassara, Ernest. "The New World of John Murray." In *"Not Hell, But Hope": The John Murray Distinguished Lectures, 1987–991*. Edited by Charles A. Howe. Murray Grove Association, 1991.

_____. "The New World of John Murray: A Character Study," *Unitarian Universalist Christian*, Vol 46, Nos. 3–4 (Fall/Winter, 1991).

Coté, Charlotte. *Olympia Brown: The Battle for Equality*. Racine, Wis.: Mother Courage Press, 1988.

Gibson, Gordon D. "The Rediscovery of Judith Sargent Murray." In *"Not Hell, But Hope."*

Howe, Charles A. "British Universalism: Elhanan Winchester, William Vidler and the Gospel of Universal Restoration." In *Transactions of the Unitarian Historical Society*, Vol. XVII, No. 1 (September 1979).

_____. "Daniel and Mary Livermore: The Biography of a Marriage." In *PUUHS*, Vol. XIX, Part II (1982–1983).

_____. "An Uneasy Alliance: Unitarians and Universalists During the Bellows Years (1839–1882)." In *PUUHS*, Vol. XXI, Part I (1987–1988).

_____. "Thomas Jefferson and Benjamin Rush: Christian Revolutionaries." In *Unitarian Universalist Christian*, Vol. 44, Nos. 3–4 (Fall/Winter, 1989).

_____. "He Lives Tomorrow: Clinton Lee Scott, Revitalizer of Universalism." In *PUUHS*, Vol. XXI, Part II (1989).

_____. "How Human an Enterprise: The First Universal Society in Boston During John Murray's Ministry." In *PUUHS*, Vol. XXII, Part I (1990–1991).

_____. "Under Orders from No Man: Universalist Women Preachers Before the Civil War." In *"Not Hell, But Hope"*, and in *Unitarian Universalism 1989: Selected Essays*. Edited by Frederick E. Gillis. Boston: Unitarian Universalist Ministers Association, 1990.

Johnson, David A. "Augusta Chapin: Universalist Pioneer, Missionary, Prophet." In *"Not Hell, But Hope."*

————. *Chicago Universalism.* Brookline, Mass.: Philomath Press, 1991.

Miller, Russell E. "A History of Universalist Theological Education." In *PUUHS*, Vol. XX, Part I (1984).

Morgan, John. "Universalized Unitarian Universalism: A Plan for Spiritual Renewal." D. Min. dissertation, Lutheran Theological Seminary, Philadelphia, Pa. 1992 (to be published by Kainos Publishing, Inc., Wilkes Barre, Pa.).

Nasemann, Raymond R., and Elizabeth M. Strong. *Remember Universalism into Life.* New York State Convention of Universalists, 1992.

New York State Convention of Universalists. *The Universalist Heritage: The Relevance of Universalism—Past, Present and Future—as Presented in Keynote Addresses to the New York State Convention of Universalists, 1976–1989* (1990).

"Not Hell, But Hope": The John Murray Distinguished Lectures, 1987–1991. Edited by Charles A. Howe. Murray Grove Association, 1991.

Robinson, David. *The Unitarians and the Universalists.* Westport, Conn.: Greenwood Press, 1985.

Saxon, A. H. *P. T. Barnum: The Legend and the Man.* New York: Columbia University Press, 1989.

————. "Olympia Brown in Bridgeport: 'Acts of Injustice' or a Failed Ministry," *PUUHS*, Vol. XXI, Part I (1987–1988).

Suffrage and Religious Principle: Speeches and Writings of Olympia Brown. Edited by Dana Greene. Metuchen, N.J.: Scarecrow Press, 1983.

The Tao of Universalism: The Thoughts, Teachings, and Writings of Dr. John Murray Atwood. Compiled by John Stewart McPhee. New York: Vantage Press, 1989.

Tucker, Cynthia Grant. *Prophetic Sisterhood: Liberal Women Ministers of the Frontier, 1880–1930.* Boston: Beacon Press, 1990.

Universalist Convocation 1990: Readings. Edited by Vernon Chandler. Gordo, Ala.: Flatwoods Free Press, 1991.

"Universalist Faith." In *Unitarian Universalist Christian*, Vol. 45, No. 1 (Spring 1990). Edited by Thomas D. Wintle.

Vreeland, Joella. *This Is the Church: The Story of a Church, a Community, and a Denomination.* First Universalist Church of Southold, New York. Mattituck, N.Y.: Amereon House, 1988.

Wright, Conrad. "A History of the Practice of Congregational Polity in Unitarian and Universalist Churches." Work in progress, 1992.

abolition of slavery, 12, 52-55, 59
Adams, Abigail, 7, 13
Adams, Frank D., 99, 107
Adams, John, 7, 13, 18
Addams, Jane, 92
Alcott, A. N., 79-80
Allen, Ethan, 18
American Congress of Liberal
  Religious Societies, 78-80
American Red Cross, 55, 100
American Unitarian Association
  (AUA), 82, 101, 119, 122, 125, 127-
  129
American Unitarian Youth, 67
*American Universalism: A Bicenten-
  nial Historical Essay*, 132-134
Andover joint assembly, 120
Association of Universalist Women
  (AUW), 68, 84, 128
associationism, 42-44
Atwood, Isaac M., 88-89, 145
Atwood, John Murray, 104
Auer, J. A. C. Fagginer, 103
Award for Distinguished Service to
  the Cause of Unitarian Universal-
  ism, 132

Baldwin, Peter, 131
Ballou, Adin, 38, 42-44, 58, 133
Ballou, Hosea, 14, 17-19, 21-47, 49,
  51, 59, 125
Ballou, Hosea 2nd, 29, 36-38, 47-49,
  51, 58, 61, 69
Banner of Love, 40
Barnum, Phineas T., 49, 58, 61, 69
Barth, Joseph, 131
Barton, Clara, 55
Bays, Carl, 127
Bellows, Henry W., 55-56, 60
Bethany Union for Young Women, 91
Bisbee, Herman, 64-65, 133
Blackmer Home (Tokyo), 84
Blair, James, 100
Bond of Fellowship and Statements
  of Faith (1935), 104-105
Boorn, Annie, 87
Boorn, George, 87

Boston Declaration (1899), 82, 103
Bowen, Henry, 35-36
Bowman, Anne, 127, 132
Brook Farm, 42
Brooks, Elbridge Gerry, 133
Brooks, Seth, 100, 111, 128
Brown, Olympia, 50, 57, 64, 69-70,
  78, 90
Bruner, Edna, 107, 132
Buchtel College, 50-51, 68
Burruss, John C., 54-56
Burton, Regina, 129

California Institute of Technology, 51
Campbell, Jeffrey, 108
Canton Theological School (see St.
  Lawrence University)
Capen, Elmer H., 78
capital punishment, 42, 58-59, 72, 90
Carnes, Paul N., 123
Cassara, Ernest, 25, 131
Cate, Isaac Wallace, 74, 83
centennial celebration, 60-62
Channing, William Ellery, 44-45, 125
Chapin, Augusta, 69, 77-78
Chapin, Edwin, 45, 69, 133
Chapman, Dorothy, 132
Charles Street Universalist Meeting
  House, 115-117
Chicago World's Fair, 77
Christ Crusade, 96,98
Christian Freeman, 40, 54
Christian Repository, 37
Christmas Day, 6-7, 31, 74, 96
Church of the Larger Fellowship,
  Unitarian Universalist, 128
Church of the Larger Fellowship,
  Universalist, 128
Civil War, 55-56, 60
Clara Barton Camp for Diabetic
  Girls, 96, 129
Cleveland, Grover, 67
Clinton Liberal Institute, 41
Cobb, Sylvanus, 40, 54, 58
Coffin, Michael, 17
Cole, David, 114-115
Commission on Social Service, 92

Committee to Study Theological
  Education, 129-130
Community Church of Boston, 97
Community Church of New York,
  102, 127-128
Cone, Orello, 90
Cook, Maria, 23-24, 56
Cope, Robert, 130
Cornish, Louis, 101, 119
Council of Liberal Churches (CLC),
  120-122
Cousens, John, 94, 97
Crane Theological School (see Tufts
  College)
Cummins, Drusilla, 132
Cummins, John, 132
Cummins, Robert, 105-109, 111-112,
  119-120, 133

Davies, A. Powell, 121
Davis, Jefferson, 55
Davis, Marguerite, 108
Dean, Paul, 30-31, 37-38
de Benneville, George, 2, 4, 10, 24, 52
Declaration of Social Principles, 92,
  96
DeWolfe, William, 132
Dimock, Marshall, 127
Divinity School Address (Ralph
  Waldo Emerson), 48
Doolittle Home, 91

Eaton, Charles, 91
Eddy, Richard, 20, 33, 47, 58, 76-77,
  133
Eliot, Frederick May, 105, 119, 125
Eliot, Samuel A., 82, 101
Emerson, Ralph Waldo, 48, 64
England, 2, 7-8
Enslin, Morton Scott, 130
Ethical Culture Society, 102
Etz, Roger, 99-100, 105
*Evangelical Magazine and Gospel
  Advocate*, 40
Everlasting Gospel, 4
Every Day Church, 91

Fay, Leon, 115
Federal Council of Churches of
  Christ in America, 108-109, 111
Ferry Beach, 76, 129
Fisher, Carleton, 112, 117-118, 121,
  127
Fisher, Ebenezer, 50

Fisher, Lewis B., 96
Fisk, Richmond, 133
"Forward Together" program, 105-
  107
Fosdick, Harry Emerson, 102
Franklin, Benjamin, 13
Fraters of the Wayside Inn, 114
Free Church Fellowship, 101-102,
  119
French, Helen, 118

Gammon, Roland, 120
Gehr, Harmon, 127, 132
General Assembly (UCA), 107-108,
  112, 114, 118-120
General Assembly (UUA), 123, 130-
  132, 135-136
General Conference of Unitarian
  Churches, 97
General Convention, 13, 22, 33, 47-
  48, 51, 53-55, 59, 61-63, 65-68, 72-
  76, 79-83, 88, 90, 92, 96, 98-101,
  103, 105, 107, 138
General Sunday School Association
  (GSSA), 96
General Superintendent, 88, 99-100,
  119-121
Genius of Truth, 40
Georgia Universalist Convention, 54
Germany, 118
Gibbons, Brainard, 112-113, 120-121
Gibson, Gordon, 135
Giles, Philip R., 121-122, 124-125,
  127, 132
Gloucester Conference, 29, 34
Gloucester, Massachusetts, 6-9, 61,
  96, 132-133
Gospel Visitant, 34-35
Grant, Ulysses S., 69
Greeley, Dana McLean, 124-125, 127-
  128
Greeley, Horace, 42, 58, 61, 69
Greene, Nicholas, 127
Greenway, Cornelius, 111, 123, 128

Hale, Edward Everett, 62
Hall, Frank Oliver, 83, 92
Harrington, Donald, 126
Harrison, Alice, 132
Harrison, Frederick, 115
Harvard Divinity School, 49, 129, 133
Henley, John Wesley, 69
Hersey, Benjamin B., 131
Holleroth, Hugo, 130

Holmes, John Haynes, 97, 102, 126
Hopedale Community, 42-44
Hopkins, Raymond, 114, 121, 127, 132
Hudson, Charles, 38
humanism, 103-104
Humanist Manifesto, 103
Humiliati, 113-115, 119, 125, 133
Hungary, 118
Hunt, James, 131, 133

Illinois State Convention, 79
Independent Church of Christ (Gloucester), 6-9, 15, 31, 52, 62
Independent Messenger, 38
Inman, James Anderson, 86
Inman's Chapel, 86-88
International Association for Religious Freedom (IARF), 83, 138
International Congress of Religious Liberals, 83

Japan mission, 74, 83-84
Jefferson, Thomas, 20
Jenkins, Lydia, 57
Jewish congregations, 79
John Murray Distinguished Lectureship, 135
Johnson, Raymond, 129
Joint Biennial Assemblies, 120
Joint Interim Committee, 115, 120
Joint Merger Commission, 115, 120, 122, 127
Jones, Jenkin Lloyd, 79
Jones, Thomas, 29
Jordan, Joseph, 75, 85
Jordan, Joseph Fletcher, 85-86
Jordan Neighborhood House, 86, 118
Joseph Priestley House, 91

Kapp, Max, 104, 121, 128, 130-132
King, Thomas Starr, 60
Klein-Nicolai, George, 4
Klotzle, Dana, 112, 118
Knapp, Arthur, 83
Kneeland, Abner, 20, 29, 44
Koishikawa Universalist Center (Tokyo), 84

Lalone, Emerson Hugh, 112
Lane, Oliver, 15
Larger Hope, The, vi, 135
Laurence, W. I., 83
Laymen's League, 96

League of Nations, 98
Liberalist, 40
Liberal Religious Youth (LRY), 67
Liberator, 54
Liberty Clause, 21, 63, 66, 82, 101, 104
Livermore, Daniel, 54-55, 58, 69
Livermore, Mary, 53-55, 58, 61, 78, 90, 133
Lockwood, Russell, 132
Lombard College (University), 50-51, 68, 100
Lowe, John Smith, 99

MacCauley, Clay, 83
MacKenzie, Helen, 118
MacLean, Angus, 109, 119, 130
MacPherson, David, 128
Madison, John, 29
Madison County, New York, 98
Massachusetts Association of Universal Restorationists, 38, 42
Massachusetts State Convention, 74, 112, 115, 117
McCollester, Lee, 94
McGinness, Mason, 112
McKeeman, Gordon, 115, 132
McKinney, Earle, 114-115, 127, 132
McLaughlin, Robert, 121
Meadville/Lombard Theological School, 50, 129-131
"Merger and Alternatives" manual and study guide, 122
Messenger of Glad Tidings, 40
Messiah Home, 91
Miller, Robert L'H., 131
Miller, Russell E., 40, 51, 55, 84-85, 89, 102-103, 125-126
Million Dollar Campaign, 96, 98
Miner, A. A., 61, 66, 84, 133
Minnesota State Convention, 64-65
missions, 67, 72-75, 83-84
Mississippi State Convention, 54
Mississippi State Department of Archives and History, 135
Mitchell, Edward, 30
Modern History of Universalism, 39
Munson, Keith, 115
Murray, John, 1-15, 17-18, 22, 24, 30-31, 34, 45, 52, 58, 60-62, 68, 72, 132-135
Murray, Judith, 8, 18, 24, 30-31, 58, 135
Murray Anniversay Crusade, 96, 98

Murray Grove, 68, 96, 129, 132, 135

Nagano Center (Japan), 118
National Conference of Unitarian
    Churches, 60-62
Netherlands, The, 118
New England Convention, 18, 20, 31,
    33, 37-38
New York State Convention, 50, 135
Nichols Academy, 41
Norfolk Mission, 75, 85
North Carolina State Convention,
    129

off-center cross, 114
Ohio State Convention, 51
Olson, Carl, 127
One Humanity, 118
Operation Bootstrap, 121
Oxford Association (1785), 77
Oxford, Massachusetts, 1, 13, 15, 77,
    96, 138
Oxnam, G. Bromley, 109

pacifism, 94, 97
Paine, Tom, 18
Parke, David, 130
Parker, Theodore, 45-46, 48
Patton, Kenneth L., 115-117, 132-133
Perin, George, 74, 78, 83, 91
Perkins, Frederic, 100, 104
Perry, Albert, 123
Philadelphia Convention, 10-14, 42,
    52
Philadelphia Convention Articles of
    Faith, 10-11, 17, 20
Pigeon River, North Carolina (see
    Inman's Chapel)
Piper, Wilson, 121
Pledge of Allegiance (Consolidation,
    1960), 126
Portsmouth, New Hampshire, 28-29
Potter, Charles Francis, 103
Potter, Thomas, 2, 4, 68, 132
Powell, Hannah Jewett, 87
Powers, Levi, 90, 92
Priestley, Joseph, 10
Primitive Expounder, 40
Principles, UUA (1959, 1985), 135-
    137
Prisoners' Friend, 59
prison reform, 42, 58-59
Pullman, George M., 90
Pullman, James M., 80

Pullman, Tracy, 111

Quakers, 59, 79, 102
Quinby, George, 72, 75

Rauschenbusch, Walter, 92
Reamon, Ellsworth C., 111, 118, 120,
    123
Reeves, Gene, 131
Reform Association (Universalist
    General Reform Association), 51-
    52, 59
Relly, James, 5-6
Restorationist Advocate, 38
Restorationists and Restorationist
    Controversy, 36-38
Rexford, Everett, 78
Rice, William, 121, 127
Rich, Caleb, 9
Rich and Poor in the New Testament,
    90
Richards, George, 15
Rogers, George, 33, 72
Rush, Benjamin, 11, 13, 52, 58-59
Ryder, William, 133
Ryder Community Center, 118
Ryder Divinity School, 50, 96

Sabellianism, 5
St. Lawrence Foundation for
    Theological Education, 130
St. Lawrence University (and
    Theological School), 50, 64, 75,
    100, 118, 129-131
Salem, Massachusetts, 29-30
Sawyer, Alan, 121, 127
Schouler, Margaret, 74, 83
Scott, Clinton Lee, 103, 111-112, 115,
    117, 127, 132
Scott, Mary Slaughter, 114-115
Scottish mission, 73-74
Scottish Universalist Convention, 73
Seaburg, Alan, vi, 131
Seaburg, Carl, 132
sesquicentennial celebration, 96
Shelter Neck, 129
Shinn, Quillen H., 67, 75, 85-86, 88-
    90, 100
Siegvolck, Paul (see Klein-Nicolai,
    Georg)
Sims, Thomas, 54
"Sister Church" program, 137
Skinner, Clarence Russell, 92-94, 96-
    98, 111, 113, 115

Smith, Stephen, 33
Smithson College, 50-51
Social Gospel, 91-92, 96, 98, 104-105
*Social Implications of Universalism,
   The,* 92, 98
Society of Universal Baptists
   (Philadelphia), 10, 13
*Some Hints Relative to the Formation
   of a Christian Church,* 14
Soule, Caroline, 68, 73
South Carolina State Convention, 53-
   54
Southern Convention, 54
Southern Pioneer, 40
Spear, Sarah, 59
Spear, Charles, 59, 69
Spencer, George, 132
Spoerl, Dorothy, 132
Stacy, Nathaniel, 20-23, 33, 72
Standard of Practical Christianity, 43
Starr King School for the Ministry,
   115, 129-130
state conventions, 33, 63, 129
Stiernotte, Alfred, 130
Streeter, Sebastian, 45
Suffolk mission, 85-86
Summer, Henry, 56
Summer Institutes, 76
Sweetser, Edwin, 75, 82, 85
Syracuse joint assembly, 123

Tapp, Robert, 130
Tar Heel Universalist, 129
Taylor, Harold, 129
Taylor Report, 129
temperance, 40, 42, 58-59, 69
Thayer, Thomas, 75
Thomas, Abel C., 66
Throop Polytechnic Institute, 51
"Transient and Permanent in
   Christianity, The" (sermon by
   Theodore Parker), 48
Transylvania, 137
Treatise on Atonement, 24-28, 34
Tribune (New York), 42
Trumpet, 39
Trumpet and Universalist Magazine,
   39-40, 56-57
Tufts College (University), 49-50, 61,
   66, 74, 92, 100, 113, 129-131
Turner, Edward, 29, 34-35, 37, 41

Ulrich, Gustav and Rebecca, 118
Ultra-Universalism, 36, 38-39, 45

Union, 5-6
Unirondack, 129
Unitarian Universalist Association
   (UUA), 1, 39, 59, 97, 115, 123, 126-
   129, 135, 137
Unitarian Universalist Church of the
   Philippines, 137
Unitarian Universalist Historical
   Society, 128
Unitarian Universalist House of the
   Joseph Priestley District, 91
Unitarian Universalist Ministers
   Association, 128
Unitarian Universalist Service
   Committee, 86, 115
Unitarian Universalist Women's
   Federation, 67, 128, 132
Unitarian Women's Alliance, 68, 128
Universalist Anti-Slavery Conven-
   tion, 53
Universalist Church of America
   (UCA), 13, 105, 108, 111, 114, 118,
   120-122, 125, 128
Universalist-Congregationalist
   relations, 45,100-102
Universalist Convention of North
   Carolina (see North Carolina State
   Convention)
Universalist Herald, 54, 56
Universalist Historical Society, 39,
   128, 133, 135
Universalist Leader, 100, 108, 112,
   122, 128
Universalist Magazine, 35-37, 39
Universalist National Memorial
   Church (Washington, DC), 99-100,
   128
Universalist Publishing House, 122
Universalist Service Committee, 84,
   112, 115, 117-118
Universalist-Unitarian relations, 44-
   45, 49, 59-60, 62, 82, 86, 101-102,
   104, 115, 119-126
Universalist Youth Fellowship, 67

van Schaick, John, 100-101, 108
Vickery, Charles, 115, 118
Voss, Carl Hermann, 130

Walnut Hill Evangelic Seminary, 42
Washburn, Israel, 61, 133-134
Washington, George, 6, 13
Washington Avowal (1935), 104-105,
   108

Weirs, The, 76
Wessels, Nils, 131
Westbrook Seminary, 41
Western Association (New York), 22-23
Western Evangelist, 40
Whittemore, Thomas, 36-39, 49, 56-58, 69, 82
Williams, George H., 95, 133-135
Willis, Annie B., 86
Winchester, Elhanan, 4, 9-14, 17-18, 22, 34, 38, 134
Winchester Profession (1803), 20-21, 38, 63, 65-66, 75, 80-82
Wise, Thomas, 85
Wolley, Robert, 121
Women's Centenary Association (WCA), 67-68, 72-75
Women's National Missionary Association (WNMA), 68, 86, 96, 107
women's rights, 42, 56-57, 59, 68-69, 90
Wood, Jacob, 35-37
Wood, John, 112
World, 39, 128
World's Parliament of Religions, 77, 82

Young, Joab, 17
Young, Owen D., 100
Young People's Christian Union (YPCU), 67, 96, 107
Young Religious Unitarian Universalists (YRUU), 67

Ziegler, Albert, 112, 115, 120, 132